PRONUNCIATION CONTRASTS IN ENGLISH

Don L. F. Nilsen

Alleen Pace Nilsen

PRENTICE HALL REGENTS
Englewood Cliffs, New Jersey 07632

To J. C. Catford

Printed in the United States of America

10 9 8 7 6

ISBN 0-13-730938-4

Prentice-Hall International (UK) Limited, *London*
Prentice-Hall of Australia Pty. Limited, *Sydney*
Prentice-Hall Canada Inc., *Toronto*
Prentice-Hall Hispanoamericana, S.A., *Mexico*
Prentice-Hall of India Private Limited, *New Delhi*
Prentice-Hall of Japan, Inc., *Tokyo*
Simon & Schuster Asia Pte. Ltd., *Singapore*
Editora Prentice-Hall do Brasil, Ltda., *Rio de Janeiro*

CONTENTS

iv

INTRODUCTION

PRONUNCIATION CONTRASTS is designed to assist teachers of English to speakers of other languages in dealing with pronunciation difficulties. It has been planned to serve as a time-saving aid for both the beginning and the experienced teacher in preparing materials for classroom use geared to the individual needs of each student. The established teacher will perhaps most appreciate being spared the hitherto tedious and time-consuming task of compiling lists of minimal pairs of words, which are now provided here in abundance. Teachers with less training or experience will find the material presented as simply as possible and that previous knowledge in this area is not presumed. A reading of this Introduction and reference to the Glossary when appropriate will readily equip the untrained teacher with the competence necessary to utilize PRONUNCIATION CONTRASTS profitably.

With regard to his students, an instructor will, of course, gain maximum efficiency from the text by isolating and concentrating on those contrasts which prove most troublesome. In many instances, these areas of difficulty are predictable because they result from 'native language interference,' in which the deeply established first language habits of the student tend to predominate until the new English speech patterns have been firmly mastered. A non-native speaker, for example, is usually able to recognize and make gross approximations of English sounds; these general approximations may, however, encompass two or three English phonemes, which the student is at first unable to differentiate. Thus, for our *th* sounds (as in *thy* and *thigh*), common to few languages aside from English, the speaker of another language tends to substitute *t, d, s,* or *z* — depending upon which of these would be likely to occur in a similar speech environment in his own tongue. Carrying over the sound he *thinks* he has heard is one of the major components of a 'foreign accent.'

The path to correction of the problem lies in contrasting the two sounds until they can be readily distinguished both in hearing and in speaking. The merit in the use of minimal pairs lies in enabling the student to study systematically those phonemes which are potentially confusing in English, rather than equip him to make technical distinctions between the sounds of English and those of his native language. In this way, the student is motivated to devote his energy and attention to his target language.

The teacher will find in this book a number of tools that should prove invaluable in accomplishing this purpose. These include: language lists designed to pinpoint those contrasts which can be expected to give trouble to various language speakers; comparative charts and diagrams of sound production; and compilations of minimal pairs of words and sentences for practice. Since stress and intonation also play a vital role in English pronunciation, the teacher should feel free to supplement drill in contrasting elements with other methods and techniques he has found helpful.

The authors have attempted to include only those basic contrasts significant to large numbers of persons learning English. In order to keep the size of the book within reasonable bounds, contrasts limited in usefulness to single language groups have not been included.

Organization of the Book

For convenience, the text is divided into three sections: the first deals with vowel contrasts; the second with consonant contrasts; and the third with multiple contrasts, including vowels and consonant clusters. The Language Index in the Appendix lists the page locations of those contrasts which are potentially difficult for speakers of the languages considered.

Consonants and vowels treated in the text appear in the following tables. To locate all the pages dealing with a particular sound, reference should be made to both the horizontal and vertical listings of the appropriate page chart.

VOWELS:

Diphthongs:

ay

aw

oy

		Front	Central	Back
High	Tense	iy		uw
	Lax	i		u
Mid	Tense	ey		ow
	Lax	e	ə	
Low	Tense	æ		
	Lax		a	ɔ

CONSONANTS:

two lips	top teeth/bottom lip	tongue tip/top teeth	tongue tip/tooth ridge	tongue tip/hard palate	tongue mid/hard palate	tongue back/soft palate	not localized	
								STOPS
p			t			k		Voiceless
b			d			g		Voiced
								CONTINUANTS
hw	f	θ	s		š		h	Voiceless
w	v	ð	z/y/l	r	ž			Voiced (Oral)
m			n			ŋ		Voiced (Nasal)
								AFFRICATES
					č			Voiceless
					j			Voiced

PAGE CHART FOR VOWELS

	i	ey	e	æ	ə	a	uw	u	ow	ɔ	ay	aw	oy
iy	1	2	3										
i		4	5	6	7								
ey			8	9	10				11				
e				12	13	14							
æ					15	16					17		
ə						18		19	20	21			
a								22	23	24	25		
u							27	28					
ow													29
aw											30		31
oy										26	32		

PAGE CHART FOR CONSONANTS

	m	p	b	hw	w	f	v	θ	ð	n	t	d	l	s	č	j	g
h				38		47											
g					42												
k																	74
ŋ	34									58						73	
y															72		
j												64					
č											61				71		
z							50		56			63		67		70	
s						46		53									
š						45		52					66	68		69	
r					41							62	65				
l										57							
d			37						55		60						
t								51									
ð							49										
θ						44			54								
v					40	43											
f		36															
w	33																
hw					39												
b	35					48											
p											59						

xi

Pronunciation

Since few English words are pronounced in precisely the same way by all native speakers of the language, contrasts which are inconsistent with the dialects of many users are bound to appear in the following lists. Kenyon and Knott's A PRONOUNCING DICTIONARY OF AMERICAN ENGLISH and THE RANDOM HOUSE DICTIONARY OF THE ENGLISH LANGUAGE have been accepted as guides, and a pronunciation listed as a standard American form in either has been included as such in PRONUNCIATION CONTRASTS. Words which are not minimal in a teacher's dialect may be excluded from his teaching list. Such non-minimal words tend to occur most frequently among low or back vowels, and among vowels followed by the so-called 'semi-consonants': /l/, /n/, /ŋ/, and especially /r/. Each of these sounds greatly influences the pronunciation of the preceding vowel, and in certain dialects the impact is more marked than in others.

The instructor should anticipate some possible difficulty in teaching a contrast which he does not naturally and consistently make. For example, the contrasts /w/-/hw/ (as in *witch-which*) and /ɔ/-/a/ (as in *caught-cot*) are differentiated in only some — but not all — sections of the United States. In teaching a contrast which he does not practice and cannot discriminate, the instructor might prefer to rely instead on an assistant to whom the contrast is natural.

Phonemic Symbols

The sounds treated in PRONUNCIATION CONTRASTS are the *phonemes* of English. Under this heading fall the significant sounds which affect meaning, as opposed to those subtle variations which constantly recur in speech. At certain points in the text, it was deemed necessary to indicate these phonemes more accurately than is possible by means of the conventional English alphabet. The symbols utilized for this purpose appear below. The sound represented is the first in heard in the example — except for a few words in which the sound is underlined.

[iy]	eat	[oy]	oil	[ð]	thy
[i]	it	[p]	pie	[s]	sip
[ey]	ate	[b]	buy	[z]	zip
[e]	any	[t]	tie	[l]	lip
[æ]	at	[d]	die	[r]	rip
[ə]	up	[k]	kite	[š]	ship
[a]	on	[g]	guy	[ž]	mea<u>s</u>ure
[uw]	b<u>oo</u>t	[hw]	which	[č]	chip
[u]	b<u>oo</u>k		(aspirated)	[j]	gyp
[ow]	own	[w]	witch	[h]	hip
[ɔ]	awning	[f]	file	[m]	mine
[ay]	aisle	[v]	vile	[n]	nine
[aw]	out	[θ]	thigh	[ŋ]	si<u>ng</u>er

Sound Production Charts

In the first two sections on vowel contrasts and consonant contrasts, each pair of contrasted sounds is presented at the top of a new page. Symbols and an example of the two sounds contrasted appear in the upper left portion of the page, one below the other. On a line with each is an exposition of its production in chart form. So that similarities and differences in production of the sounds may be seen at a glance, those production features that differ are shaded.

Profile Diagrams

The sound profile diagrams provide a graphic means of depicting the production of each sound. Like the sound production charts, they have been devised for easy comparison of the production features of the vowel or consonant pairs contrasted. The profile diagrams are designed to indicate the relative positions of lips, teeth, and tongue, the action of the vocal folds, and the uvular position which controls passage of the sound through the mouth or nasal cavity.

Vowels have been classified first, as *front, central,* or *back,* and second, as *high, middle,* or *low* — according to the height of the tongue in the mouth during the process of sound production. The chart on page viii, reproduced in the form of a grid on all vowel profile diagrams, indicates the position of the apex of the tongue when the vowel sound is produced. From the chart it can be seen, for example, that /a/ is a *low-central* vowel, /i/ is a *high-front* vowel, /e/ is *mid-front,* and /u/ is *high-back.*

Some of the contrasted vowels are actually diphthongs, that is, combinations of two vowel sounds. The solid line which appears on a profile diagram for a diphthong identifies the first vowel sound; the dotted line indicates the second.

In the profile diagrams for consonants, sounds which are *voiced* (produced by the vibration of the vocal folds) are indicated by a vibrating line. *Voiceless* sounds are depicted by a straight line.

Language Lists

The languages listed for each contrast are those whose native speakers may be expected to experience difficulty in learning the particular contrast. These lists were compiled with the assistance of more than fifty linguists and other language specialists. They serve both as a starting point for instruction and as a means of anticipating and delineating problem areas. It should be kept in mind that the specialists consulted could not reasonably be expected to anticipate individual digressions or to analyze all difficulties with uniform consistency. From this perspective, the instructor will undoubtedly decide to test each student's pronunciation at the earliest opportunity in order to isolate individual difficulties.

Sentences

Two types of sentences have been provided, each containing minimal words. The *Sentences With Contextual Clues* have been designed to permit students to hear and pronounce the contrasting sounds in their natural environment. In order to help students focus on sound distinctions, minimal words are used in stress positions whenever possible. Because of the presence of semantic clues, students will undoubtedly find these easier than the *Minimal Sentences*. In this second type, which is an extension of the minimal pairs, the entire meaning is altered by a change in a single phoneme. These sentences are valuable not only for teaching and testing auditory comprehension, but for practice in accurate sound production as well.

Lists of Minimal Pairs

A minimal pair consists of two words pronounced alike except for a single phonemic difference. This one alteration is responsible for radical changes in meaning, as in *bit-bet* or *thing-sing*. Since any sound is commonly influenced by the process of repositioning the mouth in anticipation of pronouncing the one to follow, the first word in each pair has been alphabetized according to the environment of the phoneme under study. Examples of vowel contrasts have been alphabetized by word ending, as in a rhyming dictionary; those for consonant contrasts are listed in three columns: initial, medial, and final. Where the phoneme under study is in initial position, words have been alphabetized conventionally from the beginning; where the phoneme is located in medial or final position, words have been alphabetized from the end. This method of organization, together with the provision of abundant illustrations for each contrast, should amply equip the instructor to teach any desired sound in any particular environment. Wherever possible, study of those minimal pairs in common usage should for obvious reasons receive priority. Low frequency words have been listed only for those contrasts which could not otherwise be adequately illustrated.

Pages of Multiple Contrasts

The third section of the book lists multiple contrasts of two kinds: vowels and consonant clusters. While the instructor retains the option of not working with a complete chart at one time, the contrasts have been presented in this way in order to allow greater flexibility in selection. The instructor, for instance, may decide to teach a contrast which does not appear elsewhere in the book; or he may find it advantageous to work with a multiple rather than a dual contrast. Vowels have been grouped according to similarities in production: i.e., back vowels; front vowels; diphthongs; etc. Consonant clusters have been grouped according to the sound features they have in common: clusters ending in /s/; clusters containing nasals; etc.

English consonant clusters are among the most difficult sounds for speakers of other languages to master. Although the same consonant sounds occur in many languages, they seldom occur in the same combination as in English. Practically all students, therefore, should anticipate difficulty with at least some English consonant clusters. To aid the teacher in working with these clusters, the more common ones have been arranged in groups or contrasts with single consonants, as well as with similar clusters: e.g., *gas, glass, grass.*

Some Sample Exercises

Some of the common methods of working with minimal pairs are illustrated by the following laboratory and classroom exercises dealing with the /l/-/r/ contrast. These sample drills are indicative of the many variations possible in utilizing minimal pairs:

Recognition: Number your paper from one to six. I am going to say groups of three words. Two of the words in each group will be the same. Write down the number of the word which is different. For example, if I say *quill-queer-quill,* you should write down 2, because the second word is different from the others.

1. lash-lash-rash
2. locker-rocker-locker
3. wrist-list-list
4. miles-mires-miles
5. clue-clue-crew
6. sear-seal-seal

Recognition: Number your paper from one to eight. Listen to the following words. When a word ends with /l/ write *l.* When it ends with /r/ write *r.*

1. toll
2. tore
3. toll
4. toll
5. tile
6. tile
7. tire
8. tire

Recognition: Number your paper from one to six. I will say groups of three words. Listen carefully for the word which begins with a consonant cluster containing /l/. If it is the first word in the group, write the number *1.* If it is the second word, write *2,* and if it is the third word, write *3.*

1. prod-pod-plod
2. go-glow-grow
3. flight-fright-fight
4. fame-flame-frame
5. pray-play-pay
6. blight-bite-bright

Production: Listen carefully and then repeat the following contrasts with /l/ and /r/ in initial position. Notice that /l/ words come first.

lace-race
lag-rag
lane-rain
law-raw
leap-reap
lamp-ramp

Now repeat the following contrasting words which have /l/ and /r/ in medial position.

glean-green
filing-firing
belated-berated
shield-sheared
elect-erect
collect-correct

Now repeat the following contrasting words which have /l/ and /r/ in final position.

mole-more
pole-pore
feel-fear
peal-peer
file-fire
toll-tore

Production: Listen carefully to these sentences which contain contrasts. Repeat them after me.

There is a LIGHT on the RIGHT.
The LEAF is on the REEF.
He doesn't FEEL any FEAR.
Are they FREE to FLEE?
The FILE was on FIRE.

Production: Number your paper from one to eight. Repeat the following sentences after me. If the last word begins with /l/, make a check on your paper.

1. This isn't a good lime.
2. This isn't a good rhyme.
3. This isn't a good rhyme.
4. This isn't a good lime.
5. It is a high load.
6. It is a high road.
7. It is a high load.
8. It is a high load.

Production: (If the instructor is the moderator, this can be an exercise in recognition; with a student moderator, it is an effective test of production as well.) Look at the pictures on the blackboard. Listen carefully to the following sentences and do what they tell you:

> Point to the lock.
> Point to the rock.
> Point to the rock.
> Point to the lock.
>
> Point to the rake.
> Point to the lake.
> Point to the rake.
> Point to the lake.

It is the hope of the authors that, through this book, teachers of English to speakers of other languages can at last find freedom from the drudgery of locating, codifying, and recording lists of minimal pairs, and that they may expect instead to be able to devote more of their future efforts to their main endeavor — the teaching of English.

Don L. F. Nilsen
Alleen Pace Nilsen

Acknowledgments

We gratefully acknowledge the help of those specialists who initially identi-fied potential difficulties for us. The following is a partial listing of linguists to whom we are indebted: Ahmes P. Abdel-Malik (Arabic), Edward Anthony (Thai), Emmon Bach (German), M. F. Baradja (Indonesian), Byron W. Bender (Marshallese), Charles E. Bidwell (Serbo-Croatian), Bernard Bloch (Japanese), Donald Bowen (Spanish, Tagalog, Swahili, Cebuano), William Oliver Bright (Kannada), Denzel Carr (Japanese, Hawaiian), J. C. Catford (Georgian), Yuen Ren Chao (Chinese), Heles Contreras (Spanish), Alan D. Corré (Hebrew), Joaquim De Siqueira Coutinho (Portuguese), G. A. Dhar-marajan (Tamil, Hindi), Nguyen Dinh-Hoa (Vietnamese), Charles Ekker (Portuguese), Claes-Christian Elert (Swedish), David M. Feldman (Portu-guese), Ragnar Furuskog (Swedish), Beverly K. Hall (Turkish), Robert A. Hall (Italian, Micronesian), Lars Gunnar Hallander (Swedish), Robert Thomas Harms (Russian, Estonian), Einar Haugen (Norwegian), Carleton Taylor Hodge (Persian, Hausa, Serbo-Croatian, Bulgarian), Michael Kere-sztesi (Hungarian), Masood Husain Khan (Urdu), Donald Knapp (Lebanese Arabic), Andreas Koutsoudas (Greek), Henry Kučera (Czech), Ilse Lehiste (Estonian), Herbert J. Landar (Navajo), Winfred Lehmann (German, Japa-nese), Samuel E. Martin (Korean), Eeva Kangasnaa Minn (Finnish), Choudhri Mohammed Naim (Urdu), Jacob Ornstein (Bulgarian), Alice Pack (Fijian, Samoan, Tongan), Jens Ulrich Pedersen (Danish, Swedish), James Pence (Pashto), Ernst Pulgram (French, Italian), Paul Roberts (Italian), DeLagnel Haigh Roop (Burmese), Charles August Sauer (Iranian Persian), Philip Scherer (Polish), Navine Shah (Gujarati, Tamil), George Y. Shevelov (Russian), A. L. Siddiqi (Urdu), J. Soegiarto (Javanese), Arumugam Sub-bian (Tamil), Tang The Tuong (Vietnamese), Laurence C. Thompson (Viet-namese), Hans Vogt (Georgian), W. Weinberg (Hebrew), Milton Wohl (Viet-namese), William F. Wyatt (Greek), Isabella Yiyun Yen (Chinese).

We are also grateful for the help and criticism given by Mary Lawrence of Saint Mary's College, and by John Fisher of New York State University, Col-lege at Oswego. And we are indebted to David Hoopes, Director of the Regional Council Center for International Students at The University of Pittsburgh, for allowing us to use the book experimentally during the 1965 RCCIS summer orientation program for international college students. We would especially like to thank Dr. R. Ross Macdonald, Associate Professor of Linguistics, School of Languages and Linguistics at Georgetown University, who made detailed and valuable suggestions about the presentation of this material.

The analyses, comments, and criticisms supplied by these and other lin-guists were invaluable. The authors take full responsibility, however, for the adaptation and presentation of all material in this text.

SOUND	VERTICAL POSITION	HORIZONTAL POSITION	LIP ROUNDING	DIPHTHONG-IZATION	TENSENESS
[iy] beat	high	front	unrounded	slightly diphthongized	tense
[i] bit	high	front	unrounded	not diphthongized	lax

Languages

Bulgarian
Burmese
Cebuano
Chinese
Croatian
Estonian
Fijian
French
Georgian
Greek
Hausa
Hawaiian
Hebrew
Hungarian
Indonesian
Italian
Japanese
Korean
Micronesian
Navajo
Persian
Portuguese
Russian
Samoan
Serbian
Spanish
Swahili
Swedish
Tagalog
Tamil
Thai
Tongan
Turkish
Urdu
Vietnamese

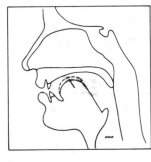
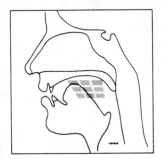

SENTENCES WITH CONTEXTUAL CLUES
Please SIT in this SEAT.
These shoes should FIT your FEET.
Do you STILL STEAL?
Those BINS are for BEANS.
They SHIP SHEEP.

MINIMAL SENTENCES
He lost the LEAD/LID.
This WEEK/WICK seems very long.
FEEL/FILL this bag.
She wore a NEAT/KNIT suit.
Don't SLEEP/SLIP on the deck.

greased-grist	deal-dill	dean-din	he's-his
keyed-kid	meal-mill	lean-Lynn	breeches-britches
steeple-stipple	real-rill	wean-win	eat-it
scheme-skim	seal-sill	sheen-shin	beat-bit
gene-gin	teal-till	keen-kin	heat-hit
case-is	steal-still	green-grin	cheat-chit
leave-live	eel-ill	seen-sin	wheat-whit
wheeze-whiz	feel-fill	teen-tin	meat-mitt
each-itch	heel-hill	heap-hip	neat-knit

bead-bid | beach-bitch | keel-kill | cheap-chip | peat-pit
lead-lid | peach-pitch | kneel-nil | leap-lip | seat-sit
deed-did | reach-rich | peel-pill | reap-rip | feet-fit
heed-hid | leak-lick | spiel-spill | deep-dip | skeet-skit
reed-rid | peak-pick | she'll-shill | sheep-ship | fleet-flit
greed-grid | teak-tick | we'll-will | jeep-gyp | sleet-slit
leafed-lift | cheek-chick | ream-rim | sleep-slip | greet-grit
skied-skid | sleek-slick | team-Tim | seep-sip | tweet-twit
creeped-crypt | seek-sick | deem-dim | sneaker-snicker | feast-fist
ceased-cyst | week-wick | bean-bin | fees-fizz | least-list
leased-list

SOUND	VERTICAL POSITION	HORIZONTAL POSITION	LIP ROUNDING	DIPHTHONG- IZATION	TENSENESS
[iy] beat	high	front	unrounded	slightly diphthongized	tense
[ey] bait	mid, becoming high	front	unrounded	diphthongized	tense

Languages

Georgian
Swedish
Urdu

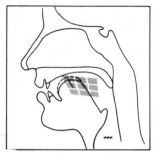 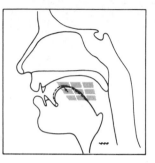

SENTENCES WITH CONTEXTUAL CLUES
I HATE this HEAT.
They SEEM the SAME.
The STREET is STRAIGHT.
The GRAIN is GREEN.
Set the TRAY under the TREE.

MINIMAL SENTENCES
We EAT/ATE at noon.
What did you SEE/SAY?
Can we maintain this PEACE/PACE?
She got the MEAL/MAIL ready.
Don't get too close to the BEE/BAY.

plea-play	Swede-swayed	weave-wave	seal-sail	keen-cane
pea-pay	bee-bay	sleeve-slave	teal-tail	green-grain
D-day	gee-jay	peeve-pave	steal-stale	seen-sane
bead-bayed	thee-they	grieve-grave	veal-vale	reap-rape
lead-laid	lee-lay	we-way	eel-ale	sheep-shape
plead-played	flee-flay	chief-chafe	feel-fail	keep-cape
mead-maid	knee-nay	beak-bake	heel-hale	creep-crepe
feed-fade	free-fray	leak-lake	wheel-whale	eat-ate
bleed-blade	spree-spray	sneak-snake	kneel-nail	heat-hate
speed-spade	tree-tray	teak-take	peel-pail	pleat-plate
reed-raid	see-say	sleek-slake	she'll-shale	meat-mate
breed-braid	siege-sage	meek-make	team-tame	peat-pate
freed-frayed	he-hay	reek-rake	deem-dame	treat-trait
greed-grade	eke-ache	seek-sake	seem-same	seat-sate
treed-trade	feeble-fable	week-wake	bean-bane	feet-fate
steed-stayed	steeple-staple	sheik-shake	dean-Dane	skeet-skate
weed-wade	me-may	deal-dale	lean-lane	sleet-slate
she'd-shade	lease-lace	meal-mail	mean-mane	greet-grate
peace-pace	grease-grace	real-rail	wean-wane	street-straight

SOUND	VERTICAL POSITION	HORIZONTAL POSITION	LIP ROUNDING	DIPHTHONG-IZATION	TENSENESS
[iy] beat	high	front	unrounded	slightly diphthongized	tense
[e] bet	mid	front	unrounded	not diphthongized	lax

Languages

Bulgarian
Burmese
Cebuano
Greek
Navajo
Tagalog
Urdu
Vietnamese

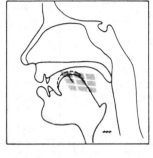 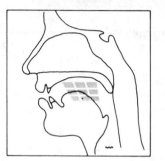

SENTENCES WITH CONTEXTUAL CLUES

Some MEN are MEAN.
The DEAN has a DEN.
The STEP is STEEP.
Will he SELL the SEAL?
We MET while buying MEAT.

MINIMAL SENTENCES

I FEEL/FELL sick.
We MEET/MET at noon.
She brings out the BEAST/BEST in him.
We FEED/FED the cat in the evening.
They BREED/BRED race horses here.

bead-bed	leaned-lend	eel-L	peep-pep
lead-led	weaned-wend	feel-fell	stoop-step
plead-pled	creased-crest	heel-hell	fees-fez
pieced-pest	lease-less	kneel-knell	sees-says
deed-dead	geese-guess	spiel-spell	seeks-sex
feed-fed	sheaf-chef	she'll-shell	beat-bet
bleed-bled	each-etch	we'll-well	wheat-whet
speed-sped	reach-wretch	steam-stem	meat-met
reed-red	speak-speck	bean-Ben	neat-net
breed-bred	cheek-check	dean-den	peat-pet
treed-tread	peek-peck	glean-glen	seat-set
seed-said	reek-wreck	mean-men	sweet-sweat
steed-stead	deal-dell	peen-pen	beast-best
weed-wed	peal-pell	teen-ten	feast-fest
leafed-left	seal-sell	beacon-beckon	least-lest
she'd-shed	teal-tell	heap-hep	priest-pressed

SOUND	VERTICAL POSITION	HORIZONTAL POSITION	LIP ROUNDING	DIPHTHONG-IZATION	TENSENESS
[i] bit	high	front	unrounded	not diphthongized	lax
[ey] bait	mid, becoming high	front	unrounded	diphthongized	tense

Languages

Arabic
Cebuano
Chinese
Indonesian
Navajo
Tagalog
Urdu

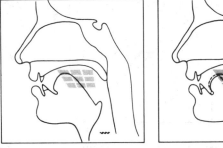
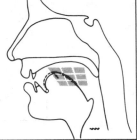

SENTENCES WITH CONTEXTUAL CLUES

I HATE to get HIT.
The PILL made her PALE.
They were LIT very LATE.
That PIN caused me PAIN.
A large STICK is a STAKE.

MINIMAL SENTENCES

It's a valuable SKILL/SCALE.
Did the man MILL/MAIL it?
They HIT/HATE him.
Take the PILL/PAIL with water.
They GIVE/GAVE it away at Christmas.

bib-babe	tick-take	trill-trail	win-wane	hit-hate
limb-lame	stick-stake	sill-sail	ship-shape	skit-skate
hissed-haste	quick-quake	till-tail	nip-nape	lit-late
bid-bayed	wick-wake	still-stale	rip-rape	slit-slate
lid-laid	nil-nail	quill-quail	drip-drape	pit-pate
slid-slayed	ill-ale	will-wail	grip-grape	spit-spate
mid-maid	bill-bale	swill-swale	tip-tape	grit-grate
rid-raid	dill-dale	dim-dame	shiver-shaver	wit-wait
grid-grade	fill-fail	bin-bane	sliver-slaver	tint-taint
wind-waned	gill-gale	fin-fain	river-raver	script-scraped
ridge-rage	hill-hale	gin-Jane	quiver-quaver	fist-faced
sieve-save	shill-shale	chin-chain	his-haze	list-laced
give-gave	skill-scale	kin-cane	trips-traipse	grist-graced
kick-cake	mill-mail	skin-skein	kiss-case	wrist-raced
lick-lake	pill-pail	pin-pane	miss-mace	tryst-traced
flick-flake	rill-rail	spin-Spain	it-ate	mitt-mate
brick-brake	frill-frail	grin-grain	bit-bait	fix-fakes
sick-sake	grill-grail	sin-sane	fit-fate	mix-makes

SOUND	VERTICAL POSITION	HORIZONTAL POSITION	LIP ROUNDING	DIPHTHONG-IZATION	TENSENESS
[i] bit	high	front	unrounded	not diphthongized	lax
[e] bet	mid	front	unrounded	not diphthongized	lax

Languages

Arabic
Bulgarian
Cebuano
Finnish
Greek
Hebrew
Italian
Javanese
Micronesian
Pashto
Persian
Swedish
Tagalog
Thai
Urdu
Vietnamese

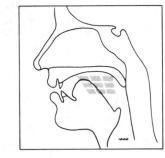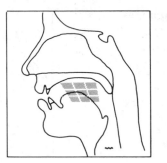

SENTENCES WITH CONTEXTUAL CLUES

He HID his HEAD.
Fasten the PIG to this PEG.
He SLID on the SLED.
Please CHECK the CHICK.
A sore WRIST needs REST.

MINIMAL SENTENCES

Hand me the PIN/PEN.
This one is BITTER/BETTER.
She showed me the LITTER/LETTER.
It was ugly because it was WITHERED/WEATHERED.
They LIFT/LEFT ten-pound weights at the gym.

disc-desk	pick-peck	tin-ten	miss-mess
sinned-send	trick-trek	hip-hep	lift-left
bid-bed	bill-bell	ear-ere	bit-bet
did-dead	dill-dell	fear-fair	whit-whet
hid-head	fill-fell	hear-hair	lit-let
lid-led	hill-hell	spear-spare	knit-net
slid-sled	shill-shell	beer-bear	pit-pet
rid-red	spill-spell	cheer-chair	sit-set
wind-wend	quill-quell	peer-pair	wit-wet
middle-meddle	sill-sell	steer-stair	wilt-welt
if-F	till-tell	whither-whether	dint-dent
big-beg	will-well	wither-weather	lint-lent
pig-peg	swill-swell	bitter-better	tint-tent
rich-wretch	him-hem	fitter-fetter	gist-jest
itch-etch	gym-gem	litter-letter	list-lest
chick-check	bin-Ben	sitter-setter	wrist-rest
flick-fleck	din-den	hicks-hex	mitt-met
nick-neck	pin-pen	bliss-bless	six-sex

SOUND	VERTICAL POSITION	HORIZONTAL POSITION	LIP ROUNDING	DIPHTHONG-IZATION	TENSENESS
[i] bit	high	front	unrounded	not diphthongized	lax
[æ] bat	low	front	unrounded	not diphthongized	lax

Languages

Burmese
Cebuano
Hebrew
Hindi
Italian
Micronesian
Swahili
Tamil
Urdu

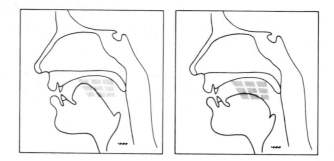

SENTENCES WITH CONTEXTUAL CLUES
That BAG is BIG.
Give the HAM to HIM.
He always THINKS to say THANKS.
This STICK is for that STACK.
If you're FAT it won't FIT.

MINIMAL SENTENCES
PICK/PACK up the bags.
He HID/HAD some money.
He nailed the STRIP/STRAP on.
I picked up the LID/LAD.
There was a RIFT/RAFT between them.

crib-crab	sling-slang	drink-drank	fiction-faction	his-has
limb-lamb	spring-sprang	shrink-shrank	friction-fraction	flicks-flax
tricked-tract	sing-sang	sink-sank	chip-chap	wicks-wax
sinned-sand	hitch-hatch	dim-dam	lip-lap	miss-mass
kissed-cast	pitch-patch	him-ham	clip-clap	shift-shaft
bid-bad	dish-dash	whim-wham	flip-flap	lift-laughed
did-dad	pith-path	slim-slam	slip-slap	rift-raft
hid-had	myth-math	rim-ram	nip-nap	drift-draft
kid-cad	lick-lack	trim-tram	snip-snap	it-at
lid-lad	slick-slack	swim-swam	rip-rap	bit-bat
mid-mad	pick-pack	gym-jam	trip-trap	fit-fat
grid-grad	trick-track	in-an	strip-strap	hit-hat
prince-prance	sick-sack	bin-ban	sip-sap	chit-chat
sieve-salve	tick-tack	fin-fan	tip-tap	kit-cat
stiff-staff	stick-stack	kin-can	chimp-champ	flit-flat
big-bag	quick-quack	skin-scan	skimp-scamp	slit-slat
jig-jag	think-thank	pin-pan	limp-lamp	pit-pat
rig-rag	blink-blank	spin-span	crimp-cramp	spit-spat
wig-wag	clink-clank	tin-tan	digger-dagger	sit-sat
zig-zag	rink-rank	fission-fashion	is-as	fist-fast

SOUND	VERTICAL POSITION	HORIZONTAL POSITION	LIP ROUNDING	DIPHTHONG-IZATION	TENSENESS
[i] bit	high	front	unrounded	not diphthongized	lax
[ə] but	mid	central	unrounded	not diphthongized	lax

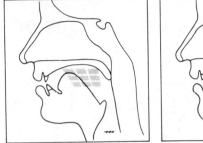 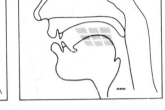

Languages

Burmese
Cebuano
Chinese
Finnish
Hebrew
Italian
Micronesian
Polish
Spanish
Tagalog
Thai

SENTENCES WITH CONTEXTUAL CLUES

Their HUT was HIT.
That STICK is STUCK.
That BUG is too BIG.
Please HUM this HYMN.
You can LICK bad LUCK.

MINIMAL SENTENCES

It was quite a STINT/STUNT.
That is a common PIN/PUN.
He had a small KIT/CUT.
They SPIN/SPUN around.
The children SWING/SWUNG on the playground.

rib-rub	sting-stung	disk-dusk	sip-sup
killed-culled	swing-swung	brisk-brusque	limp-lump
milled-mulled	pinch-punch	dill-dull	simmer-summer
bid-bud	lynch-lunch	gill-gull	this-thus
did-dud	ditch-dutch	hill-hull	kiss-cuss
kid-cud	hitch-hutch	kill-cull	miss-muss
mid-mud	chick-chuck	skill-skull	bit-but
wince-once	lick-luck	mill-mull	hit-hut
live-love	click-cluck	dim-dumb	kit-cut
sniff-snuff	pick-puck	him-hum	knit-nut
tiff-tough	trick-truck	skim-scum	pit-putt
stiff-stuff	sick-suck	slim-slum	writ-rut
big-bug	tick-tuck	rim-rum	kilt-cult
dig-dug	stick-stuck	swim-swum	hint-hunt
jig-jug	silk-sulk	bin-bun	stint-stunt
rig-rug	chink-chunk	din-done	fist-fussed
cling-clung	slink-slunk	fin-fun	gist-just
fling-flung	mink-monk	shin-shun	list-lust
sling-slung	pink-punk	pin-pun	mist-must
ring-rung	drink-drunk	spin-spun	wrist-rust
spring-sprung	shrink-shrunk	sin-sun	tryst-trust
string-strung	sink-sunk	tin-ton	mitt-mutt
sing-sung	stink-stunk	win-won	fizz-fuzz

SOUND	VERTICAL POSITION	HORIZONTAL POSITION	LIP ROUNDING	DIPHTHONG-IZATION	TENSENESS
[ey] bait	mid, becoming high	front	unrounded	diphthongized	tense
[e] bet	mid	front	unrounded	not diphthongized	lax

Languages

1 Arabic
2 Cebuano
3 Fijian
4 Georgian
5 Greek
6 Hebrew
7 Indonesian
8 Italian
9 Japanese
10 Korean
11 Micronesian
12 Navajo
13 Pashto
14 Samoan
15 Spanish
16 Swahili
17 Tagalog
18 Tamil
19 Telugu
20 Thai
21 Tongan
22 Turkish
23 Urdu
24 Uzbek
25 Vietnamese

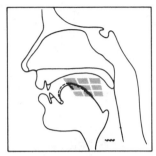 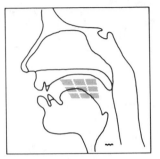

SENTENCES WITH CONTEXTUAL CLUES

Did you GET a new GATE?
Don't LET them be LATE.
Please TELL an exciting TALE.
Don't WAIT until you are WET.
We must pay our DEBT on that DATE.

MINIMAL SENTENCES

Can you TASTE/TEST it?
They will try to use LACE/LESS.
He wanted to SAIL/SELL the boat.
Put it in the SHADE/SHED.
The women make BRAID/BREAD for the tourists.

laced-lest	lace-less	tale-tell	rave-rev
raced-rest	mace-mess	flame-phlegm	ail-L
braced-breast	trace-tress	cane-Ken	bail-bell
failed-felled	fade-fed	Dane-den	fail-fell
hailed-held	shade-shed	mane-men	hail-hell
wailed-weld	blade-bled	chase-chess	jail-gel
trained-trend	spade-sped	phase-fez	nail-knell
bayed-bed	trade-tread	date-debt	quail-quell
flayed-fled	wade-wed	gate-get	wail-well
played-pled	age-edge	late-let	pain-pen
slayed-sled	wage-wedge	mate-met	rain-wren
sprayed-spread	flake-fleck	pate-pet	bacon-beckon
stayed-stead	rake-wreck	baste-best	sakes-sex
aid-Ed	bale-bell	chaste-chest	lanes-lens
laid-led	dale-dell	paste-pest	freight-fret
raid-red	shale-shell	taste-test	bait-bet
braid-bread	sale-sell	waste-west	wait-wet

SOUND	VERTICAL POSITION	HORIZONTAL POSITION	LIP ROUNDING	DIPHTHONG-IZATION	TENSENESS
[ey] bait	mid, becoming high	front	unrounded	diphthongized	tense
[æ] bat	low	front	unrounded	not diphthongized	lax

Languages

Arabic
Burmese
Cebuano
Georgian
Greek
Gujarati
Hebrew
Hungarian
Italian
Japanese
Kannada
Korean
Micronesian
Navajo
Polish
Swahili
Tagalog
Tamil
Urdu

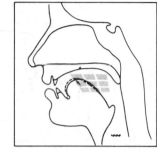 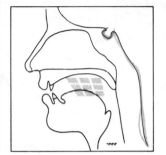

SENTENCES WITH CONTEXTUAL CLUES

I HATE this HAT.
I am MAD at the MAID.
Use BAIT to catch a BAT.
The CAP matches the CAPE.
Uncle SAM is not the SAME.

MINIMAL SENTENCES

His car has been SCRAPED/SCRAPPED.
He is the only one PAINTING/PANTING.
It is a modern PLANE/PLAN.
Please TAKE/TACK this up.
It's just a small SNAKE/SNACK.

faced-fast	paid-pad	sake-sack	pane-pan	cave-calve
laced-last	braid-brad	take-tack	cape-cap	cave-calve
paced-past	lace-lass	stake-stack	gape-gap	haze-has
baked-backed	mace-mass	quake-quack	nape-nap	pail-pal
faked-fact	pace-pass	wake-Wac	scrape-scrap	aim-am
raked-racked	brace-brass	gale-gal	tape-tap	claim-clam
grained-grand	grace-grass	shale-shall	base-bass	maim-ma'am
strained-strand	fade-fad	pale-pal	traipse-traps	fain-fan
aped-apt	glade-glad	came-cam	ate-at	Spain-span
caped-capped	made-mad	dame-dam	fate-fat	rain-ran
raped-rapt	chafe-chaff	shame-sham	hate-hat	brain-bran
taped-tapped	bake-back	lame-lamb	Kate-cat	vain-van
cased-cast	shake-shack	bane-ban	skate-scat	skein-scan
bayed-bad	lake-lack	cane-can	slate-slat	flakes-flax
played-plaid	slake-slack	Dane-dan	mate-mat	bait-bat
aid-add	snake-snack	plane-plan	rate-rat	paint-pant
laid-lad	rake-rack	mane-man	paste-past	daily-dally

SOUND	VERTICAL POSITION	HORIZONTAL POSITION	LIP ROUNDING	DIPHTHONG-IZATION	TENSENESS
[ey] bait	mid, becoming high	front	unrounded	diphthongized	tense
[ə] but	mid	central	unrounded	not diphthongized	lax

Languages

Burmese
Cebuano
Finnish
Greek
Hebrew
Navajo
Polish
Urdu

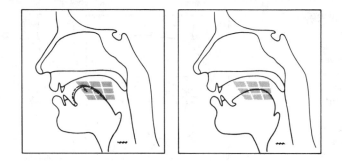

SENTENCES WITH CONTEXTUAL CLUES

I HATE this HUT.
They make such a FUSS over her FACE.
They RUN in the RAIN.
That SUM is not the SAME.
What can you GAIN with a GUN?

MINIMAL SENTENCES

That's my LAKE/LUCK.
They TRACED/TRUST her.
I saw the large CAPE/CUP.
I CAME/COME home by bus.
Only officials can go on that BASE/BUS.

laced-lust	lake-luck	wane-won	shave-shove
raced-rust	make-muck	ape-up	hail-hull
traced-trust	snake-snuck	cape-cup	mail-mull
bayed-bud	sake-suck	base-bus	nail-null
flayed-flood	take-tuck	case-cuss	maim-mum
stayed-stud	stake-stuck	phase-fuzz	feign-fun
ace-us	scale-skull	gate-gut	gain-gun
face-fuss	dale-dull	hate-hut	pain-pun
place-plus	gale-gull	Kate-cut	Spain-spun
mace-muss	came-come	slate-slut	rain-run
pace-pus	dame-dumb	mate-mutt	stain-stun
trace-truss	game-gum	pate-putt	safer-suffer
blade-blood	name-numb	rate-rut	bays-buzz
made-mud	same-sum	baste-bust	days-does
spade-spud	bane-bun	Hague-hug	straight-strut
bake-buck	Dane-done	plague-plug	bait-but
shake-shuck	sane-sun	Dave-dove	paint-punt

SOUND	VERTICAL POSITION	HORIZONTAL POSITION	LIP ROUNDING	DIPHTHONG-IZATION	TENSENESS
[ey] bait	mid, becoming high	front	unrounded	diphthongized	tense
[ow] boat	low or mid, becoming high	back	rounded, becoming more rounded	diphthongized	tense

Languages

Bulgarian
Georgian
Hebrew
Urdu

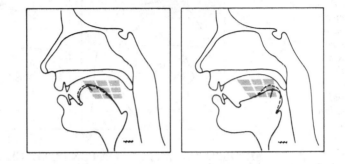

SENTENCES WITH CONTEXTUAL CLUES

Please TASTE the TOAST.
It BLOWS on the BLAZE.
Bring a CAKE and a COKE.
The GOAT broke the GATE.
A bear will DOZE for DAYS.

MINIMAL SENTENCES

The BAIT/BOAT is in the water.
Order a small CANE/CONE.
The MAIL/MOLE is in the box.
The BLAZE/BLOWS left him helpless.
There was a STAIN/STONE on the floor.

paced-post	gale-goal	raise-rose	glaze-glows	stain-stone
raced-roast	stale-stole	praise-prose	craze-crows	days-doze
cased-coast	came-comb	ate-oat	neigh-no	clays-close
aid-owed	dame-dome	date-dote	steak-stoke	slays-slows
laid-load	fame-foam	gate-goat	bail-bowl	pays-pose
maid-mode	lame-loam	mate-moat	fail-foal	bait-boat
raid-road	name-gnome	rate-wrote	hail-hole	bay-bow
grace-gross	tame-tome	baste-boast	mail-mole	day-doe
shade-showed	bane-bone	haste-host	nail-knoll	gay-go
glade-glowed	cane-cone	taste-toast	pail-pole	hay-hoe
ache-oak	lane-loan	rave-rove	rail-role	lay-low
cake-coke	sane-sewn	grave-grove	sail-soul	flay-flow
fake-folk	cape-cope	stave-stove	tail-toll	slay-slow
brake-broke	rape-rope	wave-wove	main-moan	may-mow
sake-soak	grape-grope	gaze-goes	rain-roan	ray-row
wake-woke	phase-foes	haze-hoes	drain-drone	gray-grow
dale-dole	phrase-froze	blaze-blows	grain-groan	say-so

SOUND	VERTICAL POSITION	HORIZONTAL POSITION	LIP ROUNDING	DIPHTHONG-IZATION	TENSENESS
[e] bet	mid	front	unrounded	not diphthongized	lax
[æ] bat	low	front	unrounded	not diphthongized	lax

Languages

Bulgarian
Burmese
Cebuano
Chinese
Croatian
Czech
Fijian
Finnish
Georgian
German
Greek
Gujarati
Hawaiian
Hebrew
Hungarian
Indonesian
Italian
Japanese
Javanese
Korean
Marshallese
Micronesian
Norwegian
Pashto
Persian
Polish
Portuguese
Russian
Samoan
Serbian
Spanish
Swahili
Swedish
Tagalog
Tamil
Telugu
Tongan
Turkish
Urdu
Uzbek
Vietnamese

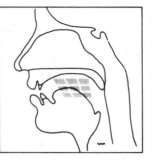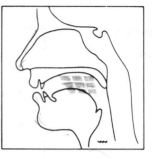

SENTENCES WITH CONTEXTUAL CLUES

This BED is BAD.
I GUESS they want GAS.
The GEM fell in the JAM.
What she SAID made me SAD.
Can you BEND this iron BAND?

MINIMAL SENTENCES

SEND/SAND it carefully.
The MEN/MAN will come.
The PEN/PAN leaks.
He got hurt on the TREK/TRACK.
She didn't want to talk about the PEST/PAST.

dead-dad	tend-tanned	then-than	pet-pat
head-had	dense-dance	men-man	set-sat
bread-brad	beg-bag	pen-pan	vet-vat
bed-bad	leg-lag	wren-ran	deft-daft
fed-fad	wrench-ranch	ten-tan	left-laughed
led-lad	flesh-flash	leather-lather	pent-pant
pled-plaid	mesh-mash	fester-faster	rent-rant
blessed-blast	thresh-thrash	better-batter	adept-adapt
messed-mast	Beth-bath	fetter-fatter	slept-slapped
said-sad	neck-knack	letter-latter	lest-last
end-and	peck-pack	less-lass	pest-past
bend-band	wreck-rack	mess-mass	guest-gassed
lend-land	trek-track	guess-gas	vest-vast
blend-bland	shell-shall	sect-sacked	X-axe
mend-manned	gem-jam	bet-bat	flex-flax
spend-spanned	hem-ham	met-mat	sex-sacks
send-sand	Ben-ban	net-gnat	

12

SOUND	VERTICAL POSITION	HORIZONTAL POSITION	LIP ROUNDING	DIPHTHONG-IZATION	TENSENESS
[e] bet	mid	front	unrounded	not diphthongized	lax
[ə] but	mid	central	unrounded	not diphthongized	lax

Languages

Arabic
Burmese
Cebuano
Chinese
Fijian
Finnish
German
Greek
Hebrew
Italian
Micronesian
Pashto
Polish
Samoan
Spanish
Tagalog
Telugu
Thai
Tongan
Urdu

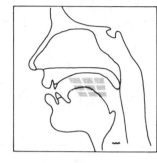 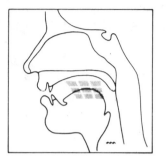

SENTENCES WITH CONTEXTUAL CLUES

They FLED from the FLOOD.
It was DONE in the DEN.
Did CHUCK get my CHECK?
A DUCK is on the DECK.
Our PUP has no PEP.

MINIMAL SENTENCES

That's an unusual NET/NUT.
Let's buy that BENCH/BUNCH.
It is only a small BED/BUD.
Are you going on a TREK/TRUCK?
The REST/RUST was orange.

dead-dud	peg-pug	Ben-bun	jet-jut
bed-bud	bench-bunch	den-done	met-mutt
decked-duct	flesh-flush	fen-fun	net-nut
bled-blood	mesh-mush	hen-Hun	pet-putt
fled-flood	thresh-thrush	pen-pun	bent-bunt
messed-must	deck-duck	wren-run	pent-punt
fend-fund	check-chuck	ten-ton	rent-runt
send-sunned	peck-puck	pep-pup	best-bust
meddle-muddle	trek-truck	hemp-hump	jest-just
peddle-puddle	desk-dusk	mess-muss	lest-lust
dense-dunce	dell-dull	sect-sucked	rest-rust
beg-bug	hell-hull	bet-but	guest-gust
leg-lug	hem-hum	get-gut	many-money

13

SOUND	VERTICAL POSITION	HORIZONTAL POSITION	LIP ROUNDING	DIPHTHONG-IZATION	TENSENESS
[e] pet	mid	front	unrounded	not diphthongized	lax
[a] pot	low	central	unrounded	not diphthongized	lax

Languages

Arabic
Cebuano
Greek
Hindi
Italian
Tamil
Urdu

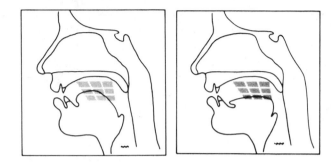

SENTENCES WITH CONTEXTUAL CLUES
Has the YACHT sailed YET?
Ships WRECK on that ROCK.
The ROD was RED.
Please STOP on the STEP.
It was NOT over the NET.

MINIMAL SENTENCES
I haven't any PEP/POP.
STEP/STOP on the line.
Leave your PET/POT with us.
He is painting the DECK/DOCK.
It was a small DEBT/DOT.

head-hod	deaf-doff	den-don	set-sot
tread-trod	beg-bog	hep-hop	wet-watt
shed-shod	keg-cog	pep-pop	yet-yacht
pled-plod	leg-log	prep-prop	**deft-doffed**
penned-pond	sketch-Scotch	step-stop	left-loft
red-rod	deck-dock	sweat-swat	adept-adopt
wed-wad	heck-hock	debt-dot	slept-slopped
said-sod	check-chock	sect-socked	crept-cropped
bend-bond	fleck-flock	get-got	swept-swapped
fend-fond	neck-knock	jet-jot	fellow-follow
blend-blonde	peck-pock	let-lot	flex-flocks
wend-wand	wreck-rock	net-not	sex-socks
ledge-lodge	dell-doll	pet-pot	jelly-jolly

SOUND	VERTICAL POSITION	HORIZONTAL POSITION	LIP ROUNDING	DIPHTHONG-IZATION	TENSENESS
[æ] bat	low	front	unrounded	not diphthongized	lax
[ə] but	mid	central	unrounded	not diphthongized	lax

Languages

Arabic
Burmese
Cebuano
Chinese
Croatian
Czech
Danish
Fijian
Georgian
German
Greek
Hausa
Hawaiian
Hebrew
Indonesian
Italian
Japanese
Micronesian
Pashto
Persian
Polish
Portuguese
Samoan
Serbian
Spanish
Swedish
Tagalog
Telugu
Tongan
Urdu

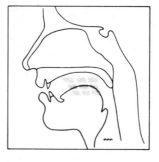

SENTENCES WITH CONTEXTUAL CLUES
My HAT is in that HUT.
The city DUMP is often DAMP.
Ducks PADDLE in this PUDDLE.
She makes RUGS from old RAGS.
Put real BUTTER in the BATTER.

MINIMAL SENTENCES
Hang the CAP/CUP on the hook.
Don't step on that BAG/BUG.
It was a real SLAM/SLUM.
It was hard to catch that BASS/BUS.
It was one of the elephant's TASKS/TUSKS.

	badge-budge	clang-clung	pack-puck	ram-rum
	rabble-rubble	slang-slung	track-truck	cram-crumb
	ramble-rumble	rang-rung	sack-suck	swam-swum
	paddle-puddle	sang-sung	tack-tuck	ban-bun
	bangle-bungle	tang-tongue	stack-stuck	fan-fun
	jangle-jungle	branch-brunch	bank-bunk	pan-pun
	ankle-uncle	hatch-hutch	dank-dunk	span-spun
cab-cub	rapture-rupture	match-much	flank-flunk	ran-run
dab-dub	plaque-pluck	graph-gruff	plank-plunk	tan-ton
flab-flub	staff-stuff	gash-gush	spank-spunk	sadden-sudden
nab-nub	calf-cuff	hash-hush	drank-drunk	cap-cup
grab-grub	half-huff	lash-lush	shrank-shrunk	damp-dump
tab-tub	bag-bug	flash-flush	sank-sunk	lamp-lump
stab-stub	hag-hug	slash-slush	mask-musk	clamp-clump
bad-bud	jag-jug	mash-mush	task-tusk	ramp-rump
cad-cud	lag-lug	rash-rush	gal-gull	stamp-stump
dad-dud	slag-slug	brash-brush	gravel-grovel	adder-udder
mad-mud	snag-snug	crash-crush	ma'am-mum	pamper-pumper
gassed-gust	rag-rug	thrash-thrush	cam-come	flatter-flutter
sand-sunned	drag-drug	back-buck	dam-dumb	patter-putter
stand-stunned	tag-tug	shack-shuck	ham-hum	bass-bus
dance-dunce	hang-hung	lack-luck	slam-slum	mass-muss

15

SOUND	VERTICAL POSITION	HORIZONTAL POSITION	LIP ROUNDING	DIPHTHONG-IZATION	TENSENESS
[æ] cat	low	front	unrounded	not diphthongized	lax
[a] cot	low	central	unrounded	not diphthongized	lax

Languages

Almost all EFL students will have some difficulty with this contrast.

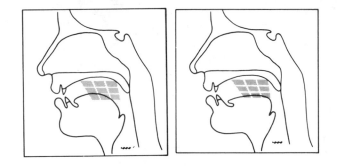

SENTENCES WITH CONTEXTUAL CLUES

That AD is ODD.
The COP wore a CAP.
It's too HOT for a HAT.
Take STOCK of that STACK.
She SANG a SONG.

MINIMAL SENTENCES

My SACK/SOCK is torn.
That MAP/MOP is too old.
I fell over the RACK/ROCK.
It is in his PACKET/POCKET.
The room is full of CATS/COTS.

cab-cob	hag-hog	sack-sock	tags-togs
gab-gob	jag-jog	tack-tock	backs-box
jab-job	lag-log	stack-stock	packs-pox
lab-lob	flag-flog	mask-mosque	cat-cot
blab-blob	batch-botch	ma'am-mom	scat-Scot
slab-slob	slash-slosh	pram-prom	hat-hot
nab-knob	flak-flock	an-on	slat-slot
cad-cod	back-bock	can-con	gnat-not
had-hod	hack-hock	Dan-don	pat-pot
clad-clod	shack-shock	cap-cop	spat-spot
pad-pod	lack-lock	chap-chop	rat-rot
sad-sod	black-block	lap-lop	sat-sot
add-odd	clack-clock	flap-flop	packet-pocket
plaid-plod	knack-knock	slap-slop	racket-rocket
band-bond	smack-smock	map-mop	daft-doffed
bland-blonde	pack-pock	pap-pop	fallow-follow
axe-ox	rack-rock	sap-sop	lax-locks
bag-bog	crack-crock	tap-top	flax-flocks

SOUND	VERTICAL POSITION	HORIZONTAL POSITION	LIP ROUNDING	DIPHTHONG-IZATION	TENSENESS
[æ] bat	low	front	unrounded	not diphthongized	lax
[ay] bite	low, becoming high	central, becoming front	unrounded	greatly diphthongized	tense

Languages

Burmese
Chinese
Georgian
Greek
Hebrew
Navajo
Pashto
Polish
Urdu

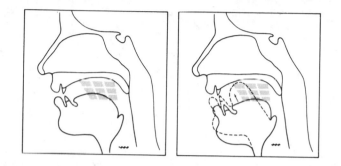

SENTENCES WITH CONTEXTUAL CLUES

Put BACK my BIKE.
The MAN is in the MINE.
They SAT at the SITE.
Is that the LAD who LIED?
It is FINE to bring a FAN.

MINIMAL SENTENCES

The man FANNED/FINED her.
It was SAND/SIGNED.
They HAD/HIDE it here.
That's a big MAN/MINE.
He began to CLAM/CLIMB up.

jab-jibe	hand-hind	ram-rhyme	ass-ice
lamb-lime	land-lined	gram-grime	lass-lice
bad-bide	grand-grind	fan-fine	mass-mice
dad-died	sand-signed	man-mine	bat-bite
gad-guide	have-hive	Nan-nine	cat-kite
had-hide	laugh-life	pan-pine	fat-fight
lad-lied	back-bike	span-spine	hat-height
glad-glide	hack-hike	bran-brine	flat-flight
brad-bride	lack-like	tan-tine	slat-slight
sad-side	pack-pike	van-vine	mat-might
add-I'd	track-trike	snap-snipe	gnat-night
canned-kind	tack-tyke	pap-pipe	spat-spite
fanned-find	pal-pile	rap-ripe	rat-right
manned-mind	am-I'm	trap-tripe	brat-bright
panned-pined	dam-dime	strap-stripe	sat-sight
plaid-plied	clam-climb	tap-type	pant-pint
band-bind	slam-slime	as-eyes	lax-likes

SOUND	VERTICAL POSITION	HORIZONTAL POSITION	LIP ROUNDING	DIPHTHONG-IZATION	TENSENESS
[ə] cut	mid	central	unrounded	not diphthongized	lax
[a] cot	low	central	unrounded	not diphthongized	lax

Languages

Arabic
Burmese
Cebuano
Chinese
Croatian
Czech
Danish
Estonian
Fijian
Finnish
Georgian
Greek
Hausa
Hebrew
Hindi
Hungarian
Italian
Japanese
Javanese
Marshallese
Micronesian
Norwegian
Persian
Polish
Russian
Samoan
Serbian
Spanish
Swahili
Swedish
Tagalog
Tamil
Thai
Tongan
Turkish
Vietnamese

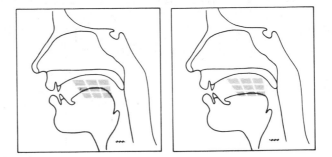

SENTENCES WITH CONTEXTUAL CLUES

I hope that's NOT a NUT.
That HUT was certainly HOT.
I hate to SLOSH through this SLUSH.
Hand this CUP to the COP.
Is that a DUCK on the DOCK?

MINIMAL SENTENCES

The new design was MUDDLED/MODELED.
The RUBBER/ROBBER is there.
That's my LUCK/LOCK.
The CUB/COB is under the table.
He gave me a HUG/HOG.

	nuzzle-nozzle	luck-lock	sculler-scholar
	come-calm	cluck-clock	sputter-spotter
	one-wan	muck-mock	suds-sods
	done-don	puck-pock	bucks-box
	none-non	suck-sock	pucks-pox
	scuff-scoff	stuck-stock	sups-sops
	gulf-golf	dull-doll	duct-docked
	bug-bog	lull-loll	cut-cot
	hug-hog	mull-moll	gut-got
cub-cob	jug-jog	bum-bomb	hut-hot
hub-hob	smug-smog	mum-mom	shut-shot
snub-snob	tug-tog	pump-pomp	jut-jot
rub-rob	crutch-crotch	rump-romp	slut-slot
sub-sob	gush-gosh	stump-stomp	nut-not
punned-pond	slush-slosh	cup-cop	putt-pot
fund-fond	buck-bock	pup-pop	rut-rot
cud-cod	duck-dock	sup-sop	flux-flocks
cuddle-coddle	chuck-chock	rubber-robber	crux-crocks
muddle-model	shuck-shock	udder-odder	nubby-knobby

SOUND	VERTICAL POSITION	HORIZONTAL POSITION	LIP ROUNDING	DIPHTHONG-IZATION	TENSENESS
[ə] buck	mid	central	unrounded	not diphthongized	lax
[u] book	high	back	rounded	not diphthongized	lax

Languages

Bulgarian
Burmese
Cebuano
Chinese
Fijian
Finnish
Greek
Hebrew
Japanese
Polish
Portuguese
Samoan
Spanish
Tagalog
Thai
T'ongan
Vietnamese

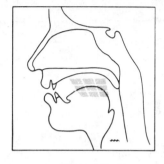 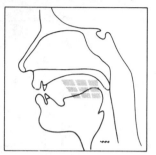

SENTENCES WITH CONTEXTUAL CLUES
The BOOK cost a BUCK.
The tailor TOOK a TUCK.
It is good LUCK to LOOK.
It doesn't LOOK like good LUCK.
He told HUCK to help find the HOOK.

MINIMAL SENTENCES
Jan had two BUCKS/BOOKS.
They were HUCK'S/HOOKS.
They SHUCK/SHOOK the farmer's corn.
He PUTTS/PUTS golf balls into the cup.
They TUCK/TOOK up the extra.

cud-could
stud-stood
huff-hoof
buck-book
Huck-hook
shuck-shook
luck-look
snuck-snook
ruck-rook
tuck-took
stuck-stook
putt-put
crux-crooks

SOUND	VERTICAL POSITION	HORIZONTAL POSITION	LIP ROUNDING	DIPHTHONG-IZATION	TENSENESS
[ə] but	mid	central	unrounded	not diphthongized	lax
[ow] boat	low or mid, becoming high	back	rounded, becoming more rounded	diphthongized	tense

Languages

Arabic
Bulgarian
Burmese
Cebuano
Greek
Hebrew
Hindi
Navajo
Polish
Portuguese
Tagalog
Tamil
Thai
Urdu
Vietnamese

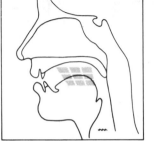 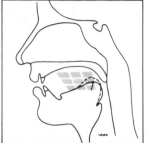

SENTENCES WITH CONTEXTUAL CLUES

He MUST have the MOST.
Has your COAT been CUT?
Please COME and bring a COMB.
It FLOWED because of the FLOOD.
The HOLES are full of HULLS.

MINIMAL SENTENCES

He was given a NUT/NOTE.
It was an ugly CUT/COAT.
It will RUST/ROAST quickly.
The artist made quite a BUST/BOAST.
The little boy is SUCKING/SOAKING his thumb.

dumb-dome	chuck-choke	ton-tone	gust-ghost
numb-gnome	cluck-cloak	bun-bone	must-most
crumb-chrome	puck-poke	fun-phone	rust-roast
rub-robe	suck-soak	Hun-hone	mutt-moat
cussed-coast	struck-stroke	shun-shone	but-boat
flood-flowed	stuck-stoke	nun-known	cut-coat
bud-bowed	cull-coal	pun-pone	gut-goat
cud-code	dull-dole	run-roan	smut-smote
mud-mode	gull-goal	sun-sewn	nut-note
crud-crowed	hull-hole	stun-stone	rut-wrote
stud-stowed	mull-mole	cup-cope	crux-croaks
come-comb	null-knoll	pup-pope	buggy-bogey
none-known	hum-home	does-doze	buzz-bows
rug-rogue	rum-roam	bust-boast	fuzz-foes

SOUND	VERTICAL POSITION	HORIZONTAL POSITION	LIP ROUNDING	DIPHTHONG-IZATION	TENSENESS
[ə] but	mid	central	unrounded	not diphthongized	lax
[ɔ] bought	low	back	slightly rounded	not diphthongized	lax

Languages

Arabic
Burmese
Cebuano
Chinese
Croatian
Czech
Fijian
Finnish
Georgian
Greek
Hebrew
Hindi
Hungarian
Indonesian
Italian
Japanese
Javanese
Korean
Micronesian
Persian
Polish
Samoan
Serbian
Spanish
Swahili
Swedish
Tagalog
Tamil
Thai
Tongan
Urdu

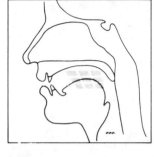 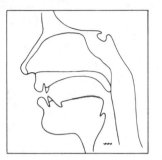

SENTENCES WITH CONTEXTUAL CLUES

It was DUG by the DOG.
I can't LUG a LOG.
It was DONE at DAWN.
My GUN is GONE.
Tell CHUCK to bring the CHALK.

MINIMAL SENTENCES

They were both CUT/CAUGHT.
That's no FUN/FAWN.
Can you TUCK/TALK this up?
They are HUNTING/HAUNTING an old castle.
Is it DONE/DAWN yet?

dub-daub	lung-long	cull-call	ruckus-raucus
sculled-scald	wrung-wrong	gull-gall	hunt-haunt
cussed-cost	sung-song	hull-hall	bust-bossed
flood-flawed	dug-dog	mull-maul	lust-lost
bud-bawd	hunch-haunch	fun-fawn	crust-crossed
cud-cawed	lunch-launch	pun-pawn	but-bought
thud-thawed	punch-paunch	spun-spawn	cut-caught
mud-Maude	buck-balk	sun-sawn	nut-nought
bubble-bauble	chuck-chalk	cruller-crawler	rut-wrought
done-dawn	tuck-talk	muss-moss	tut-taught
cuff-cough	stuck-stalk	bus-boss	buddy-bawdy

SOUND	VERTICAL POSITION	HORIZONTAL POSITION	LIP ROUNDING	DIPHTHONG- IZATION	TENSENESS
[a] pot	low	central	unrounded	not diphthongized	lax
[u] put	high	back	rounded	not diphthongized	lax

Languages

Burmese
Hebrew
Hindi
Hungarian
Italian
Micronesian
Portuguese
Tamil
Urdu

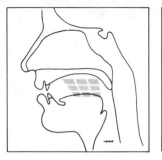 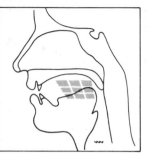

SENTENCES WITH CONTEXTUAL CLUES
It COULD be COD.
He PUT down the POT.
Please LOOK at my LOCK.
I want a BOOK about BACH.
The CROOK stole my CROCK.

MINIMAL SENTENCES
The cowboy COCKED/COOKED it.
The boy played HOCKEY/HOOKY.
LOCK/LOOK it up in the library.
Can you POT/PUT the flowers here?
You SHOCK/SHOOK him.

wad-would	knock-nook
cod-could	rock-rook
god-good	crock-crook
hod-hood	tock-took
shod-should	pot-put
posse-pussy	sot-soot
botch-Butch	box-books
posh-push	cocky-cookie
cock-cook	hockey-hooky
hock-hook	rocky-rookie
shock-shook	folly-fully
lock-look	Polly-pulley

22

SOUND	VERTICAL POSITION	HORIZONTAL POSITION	LIP ROUNDING	DIPHTHONG-IZATION	TENSENESS
[a] cot	low	central	unrounded	not diphthongized	lax
[ow] coat	low or mid, becoming high	back	rounded, becoming more rounded	diphthongized	tense

Languages

Arabic
Bulgarian
Burmese
Cebuano
Chinese
Estonian
Georgian
Greek
Hebrew
Hindi
Hungarian
Italian
Japanese
Micronesian
Navajo
Norwegian
Pashto
Portuguese
Spanish
Swahili
Swedish
Tagalog
Tamil
Thai
Turkish
Urdu
Vietnamese

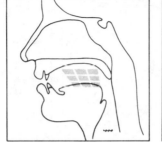
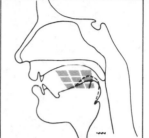

SENTENCES WITH CONTEXTUAL CLUES
I HOPE you can HOP.
It's NOT in the NOTE.
Who's GOT your GOAT?
Did JOHN invite JOAN?
Hang the CLOAK under the CLOCK.

MINIMAL SENTENCES
That COT/COAT is too small.
That was his last HOP/HOPE.
He hadn't seen the SMOCK/SMOKE.
Give it to JOHN/JOAN.
He looked at the CLOCK/CLOAK.

lob-lobe	cock-coke	John-Joan	cot-coat
glob-globe	chock-choke	con-cone	dot-dote
rob-robe	block-bloke	cop-cope	got-goat
odd-owed	clock-cloak	hop-hope	shot-shoat
bond-boned	smock-smoke	slop-slope	blot-bloat
cod-code	pock-poke	mop-mope	not-note
god-goad	crock-croak	pop-pope	rot-wrote
hod-hoed	sock-soak	sop-soap	tot-tote
shod-showed	doll-dole	cocks-coax	ox-oaks
nod-node	moll-mole	hocks-hoax	fox-folks
rod-road	calm-comb	loft-loafed	pox-pokes
sod-sewed	Tom-tome	want-won't	holly-holy

SOUND	VERTICAL POSITION	HORIZONTAL POSITION	LIP ROUNDING	DIPHTHONG-IZATION	TENSENESS
[a] cot	low	central	unrounded	not diphthongized	lax
[ɔ] caught	low	back	slightly rounded	not diphthongized	lax

Languages

Arabic
Cebuano
Chinese
Croatian
Czech
Fijian
Georgian
German
Greek
Gujarati
Hawaiian
Hungarian
Japanese
Kannada
Korean
Persian
Polish
Portuguese
Russian
Samoan
Serbian
Spanish
Swedish
Tagalog
Tongan
Turkish
Urdu
Vietnamese

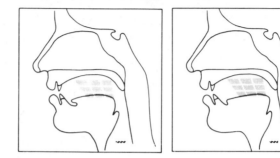

SENTENCES WITH CONTEXTUAL CLUES

Her skirt CAUGHT on the COT.
He TAUGHT the little TOT.
It did NOT come to NOUGHT.
The police SOUGHT the miserable SOT.
It was CHOCK full of CHALK.

MINIMAL SENTENCES

Is it DON/DAWN?
Spell the word POND/PAWNED.
It was SOD/SAWED in the yard.
He paid $100 for the STOCKS/STALKS.
Write the word ROT/WROUGHT.

ma-maw
odd-awed
fond-fawned
pond-pawned
cod-cawed
hod-hawed
clod-clawed
nod-gnawed
pod-pawed
sod-sawed
guard-gored
bobble-bauble
are-or
ah-awe
rah-raw
bock-balk
cock-caulk

hock-hawk
chock-chalk
tock-talk
stock-stalk
moll-maul
don-dawn
collar-caller
holler-hauler
popper-pauper
slotter-slaughter
bot-bought
cot-caught
not-naught
rot-wrought
sot-sought
tot-taught
body-bawdy

SOUND	VERTICAL POSITION	HORIZONTAL POSITION	LIP ROUNDING	DIPHTHONG-IZATION	TENSENESS
[a] dot	low	central	unrounded	not diphthongized	lax
[aw] doubt	low, becoming high	central, becoming back	unrounded, becoming rounded	greatly diphthongized	tense

Languages

Arabic
Burmese
Chinese
Hebrew
Hindi
Japanese
Navajo
Portuguese
Tamil
Turkish
Urdu

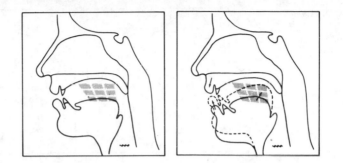

SENTENCES WITH CONTEXTUAL CLUES
Don't PROD PROUD people.
Did DON fall DOWN?
The CLOUT caused a CLOT.
He is BOUND to buy a BOND.
I heard a SHOUT followed by a SHOT.

MINIMAL SENTENCES
It is only a small SPOT/SPOUT.
He went to the POND/POUND.
Did you hear that SHOT/SHOUT?
Hurry DON/DOWN.
Any good SCOT/SCOUT knows that.

pa-pow
wand-wound
bond-bound
fond-found
pond-pound
trond-trowned
cod-cowed
clod-cloud
plod-plowed
prod-proud
gone-gown
are-hour
bronze-browns
crotch-crouch

don-down
scholar-scowler
bot-bout
Scot-scout
dot-doubt
got-gout
shot-shout
lot-lout
clot-clout
pot-pout
spot-spout
rot-rout
trot-trout
tot-tout

25

SOUND	VERTICAL POSITION	HORIZONTAL POSITION	LIP ROUNDING	DIPHTHONG-IZATION	TENSENESS
[ɔ] ball	low	back	slightly rounded	not diphthongized	lax
[oy] boil	low, becoming high	back, becoming front	rounded, becoming unrounded	greatly diphthongized	tense

Languages

Burmese
Cebuano
Hindi
Javanese
Navajo
Tamil
Urdu

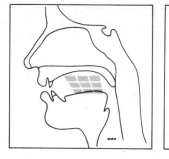
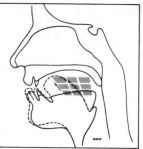

SENTENCES WITH CONTEXTUAL CLUES
Can ROY eat it RAW?
Did he FALL on the FOIL?
One quart of OIL is ALL.
Will you CALL about the COIL?
She was POISED as she PAUSED.

MINIMAL SENTENCES
Do you need ALL/OIL?
It was a strange FALL/FOIL.
He got a CALL/COIL.
It sounds like it's BAWLING/BOILING.
I could hear the neighbors BRAWLING/BROILING.

flawed-Floyd
bald-boiled
pause-poise
cough-coif
all-oil
call-coil
fall-foil
spall-spoil
tall-toil
bawl-boil

brawl-broil
lawn-loin
gnaws-noise
jaunt-joint
caw-coy
jaw-joy
claw-cloy
paw-poi
raw-Roy
saw-soy

SOUND	VERTICAL POSITION	HORIZONTAL POSITION	LIP ROUNDING	DIPHTHONG- IZATION	TENSENESS
[u] pull	high	back	rounded	not diphthongized	lax
[uw] pool	high	back	greatly rounded	slightly diphthongized	tense

Languages

Bulgarian
Burmese
Cebuano
Chinese
Croatian
Czech
Fijian
French
Georgian
Greek
Hebrew
Hindi
Hungarian
Indonesian
Italian
Micronesian
Navajo
Persian
Samoan
Serbian
Spanish
Swahili
Swedish
Tagalog
Tamil
Tongan
Turkish
Urdu
Vietnamese

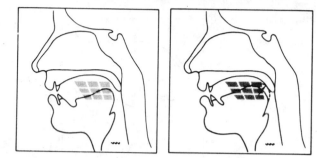

SENTENCES WITH CONTEXTUAL CLUES

Please take a LOOK at LUKE.
That FOOL is never FULL.
But SHOULD a horse be SHOED?
Did you PULL him into the POOL?
The pigeon COULD have COOED.

MINIMAL SENTENCES

They are PULLING/POOLING it.
He said the pigeon COULD/COOED.
She STOOD/STEWED them in the kitchen.
Only a FULL/FOOL horse would do it.
Did you read it in LOOK/LUKE?

could-cooed
should-shoed
would-wooed
good-gooed
hood-who'd
stood-stewed
look-Luke
full-fool
pull-pool

27

SOUND	VERTICAL POSITION	HORIZONTAL POSITION	LIP ROUNDING	DIPHTHONG- IZATION	TENSENESS
[u] could	high	back	rounded	not diphthongized	lax
[ow] code	low or mid, becoming high	back	rounded, becoming more rounded	diphthongized	tense

Languages

Bulgarian
Croatian
Georgian
Hindi
Italian
Micronesian
Serbian
Spanish
Tamil
Urdu

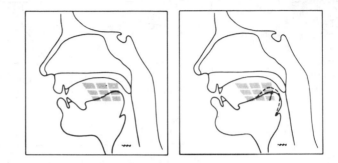

SENTENCES WITH CONTEXTUAL CLUES

That FOAL is very FULL.
It BROKE in the BROOK.
That COULD be the CODE.
Please PULL on the POLE.
Will the COOK bring me a COKE?

MINIMAL SENTENCES

I saw a red BULL/BOWL.
It sounded like a CROOK/CROAK.
The COOK/COKE is in the kitchen.
The sailor PULLED/POLED the raft.
She STOOD/STOWED it in the corner.

could-code
should-showed
good-goad
hood-hoed
stood-stowed
cook-coke
brook-broke
crook-croak
bull-bowl
full-foal
pull-pole
hooks-hoax

SOUND	VERTICAL POSITION	HORIZONTAL POSITION	LIP ROUNDING	DIPHTHONG-IZATION	TENSENESS
[ow] bowl	low or mid, becoming high	back	rounded, becoming more rounded	diphthongized	tense
[oy] boil	low, becoming high	back, becoming front	rounded, becoming unrounded	greatly diphthongized	tense

Languages

Gujarati
Hebrew
Hindi
Javanese
Navajo
Tamil

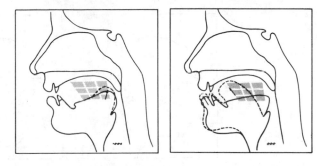

SENTENCES WITH CONTEXTUAL CLUES
Will JOAN get to JOIN?
That BOY is her BEAU.
He TOLD how they TOILED.
Toss the COIN into the CONE.
At the MOST they will only be MOIST.

MINIMAL SENTENCES
Is the girl POSED/POISED?
It's good for the SOUL/SOIL.
Are they still BOWLING/BOILING?
This COAL/COIL is unsatisfactory.
A good HOST/HOIST will keep things moving.

load-Lloyd
toad-toyed
posed-poised
bowed-buoyed
flowed-Floyd
old-oiled
bold-boiled
cold-coiled
fold-foiled
sold-soiled
told-toiled
cone-coin
Joe-joy
toe-toy
nose-noise
pose-poise

quote-quoit
coal-coil
foal-foil
roll-roil
toll-toil
soul-soil
bowl-boil
Joan-join
loan-loin
groan-groin
so-soy
host-hoist
most-moist
bow-boy
row-Roy
tow-toy

SOUND	VERTICAL POSITION	HORIZONTAL POSITION	LIP ROUNDING	DIPHTHONG-IZATION	TENSENESS
[aw] bout	low, becoming high	central, becoming back	unrounded, becoming rounded	greatly diphthongized	tense
[ay] bite	low, becoming high	central, becoming front	unrounded	greatly diphthongized	tense

Languages

Hebrew
Urdu

SENTENCES WITH CONTEXTUAL CLUES
She CRIED to the CROWD.
He LIED out LOUD.
He SIGNED without a SOUND.
It turned BROWN in the BRINE.
He's PROUD of his son's PRIDE.

MINIMAL SENTENCES
Let's go DOWN/DINE.
Bring the white MOUSE/MICE.
The best players FOULED/FILED out.
The chef DOUSED/DICED the vegetables.
The Indians GROUND/GRIND corn.

bound-bind
found-find
hound-hind
mound-mind
round-rind
ground-grind
sound-signed
wound-wind
loud-lied
proud-pride
crowd-cried
douse-dice

louse-lice
mouse-mice
spouse-spice
rouse-rise
drowse-dries
bough-buy
foul-file
owl-isle
noun-nine
down-dine
brown-brine
town-tine

chowder-chider
bower-buyer
shower-shyer
power-pyre
tower-tire
our-ire
flour-flier
sour-sire
oust-iced
bout-bite
lout-light
spout-spite

rout-right
sprout-sprite
trout-trite
tout-tight
bow-by
scow-sky
how-hi
now-nigh
plow-ply
prow-pry
sow-sigh
vow-vie

SOUND	VERTICAL POSITION	HORIZONTAL POSITION	LIP ROUNDING	DIPHTHONG-IZATION	TENSENESS
[aw] bough	low, becoming high	central, becoming back	unrounded, becoming rounded	greatly diphthongized	tense
[oy] boy	low, becoming high	back, becoming front	rounded, becoming unrounded	greatly diphthongized	tense

Languages

Burmese
Hebrew
Javanese
Navajo
Tamil
Urdu

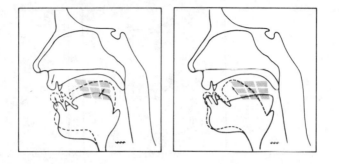

SENTENCES WITH CONTEXTUAL CLUES
That BOY didn't BOW.
An OWL likes OIL.
He fed SOY to the SOW.
Our plans were FOILED when he FOULED.
The COW seemed almost COY.

MINIMAL SENTENCES
That is FOUL/FOIL.
I found the OWL/OIL.
He rolled it into a COWL/COIL.
I noticed the unusual BOUGH/BOY.
The farmer is building a shed for his SOW/SOY

vowed-void
avowed-avoid
loud-Lloyd
cloud-cloyed
jounce-joints
pounce-points
bough-boy
foul-foil
owl-oil
cowl-coil
joust-joist
cow-coy
plow-ploy
pow-poi
row-Roy
sow-soy

SOUND	VERTICAL POSITION	HORIZONTAL POSITION	LIP ROUNDING	DIPHTHONG-IZATION	TENSENESS
[oy] boy	low, becoming high	back, becoming front	rounded, becoming unrounded	greatly diphthongized	tense
[ay] buy	low, becoming high	central, becoming front	unrounded	greatly diphthongized	tense

Languages

Arabic
Burmese
Cebuano
Hausa
Hindi
Javanese
Navajo
Tamil
Urdu

SENTENCES WITH CONTEXTUAL CLUES
It was ROY who wanted RYE.
We'll TRY to visit TROY.
Please POINT to the PINT.
Was it LLOYD who LIED?
They COINED the wrong KIND.

MINIMAL SENTENCES
He gave me a TOY/TIE.
That's a good BOY/BUY.
Their plans were FOILED/FILED.
The girl has POISE/PIES.
They are TOILING/TILING in the new house.

coined-kind
void-vied
Lloyd-lied
voice-vice
poise-pies
oil-isle
boil-bile
foil-file
roil-rile
toil-tile
loin-line
loiter-lighter

foyer-fire
lawyer-liar
Roy's-rise
quoit-quite
point-pint
hoist-heist
boy-buy
alloy-ally
ploy-ply
Roy-rye
Troy-try
toy-tie

SOUND	VOICING	DURATION	PASSAGE	ARTICULATOR	POINT OF ARTICULATION
[m] Mac	voiced	continuant	nasal	lower lip	upper lip
[w] Wac	voiced	continuant	oral	lower lip	upper lip (lips are tightly rounded)

Languages

Bulgarian
Danish
Hebrew
Hindi
Micronesian
Tamil
Urdu

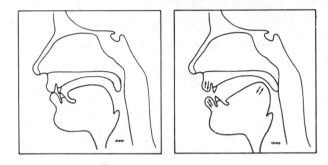

SENTENCES WITH CONTEXTUAL CLUES

(init.)   That WINE is MINE.
        It is WORN by those who MOURN.
        He made a WAGER about the MAJOR.
(med.) REMIND her to REWIND the clock.
(fin.)   The BLOOM was BLUE.

MINIMAL SENTENCES

(init.)   The party was MILD/WILD.
        The horse was caught in the MIRE/WIRE.
        He MEANT/WENT to do it.
(med.) The picture was GLOOMY/GLUEY.
(fin.)   The DOME/DOUGH burned.

initial			
made-wade	mean-wean	minnow-winnow	homing-hoeing
mail-wail	meant-went	minter-winter	gloomy-gluey
major-wager	measles-weasles	mire-wire	
make-wake	meek-week	mirth-worth	
malt-Walt	melt-welt	mitt-wit	
mane-wane	mend-wend	mix-wicks	*final*
mangle-wangle	mere-we're	mood-wooed	dome-dough
mare-ware	messed-west	mound-wound	foam-foe
mate-wait	met-wet	mourn-worn	loam-low
maul-wall	mild-wild	myth-with	doom-do
may-way	mile-wile		loom-lieu
maze-ways	mill-will		bloom-blue
me-we	mince-wince	*medial*	gloom-glue
mead-weed	mind-wind	dismayed-dissuade	room-rue
meal-we'll	mine-wine	remind-rewind	broom-brew
	mink-wink	chroming-crowing	groom-grew

SOUND	VOICING	DURATION	PASSAGE	ARTICULATOR	POINT OF ARTICULATION
[m] ham	voiced	continuant	nasal	lower lip	upper lip
[ŋ] hang	voiced	continuant	nasal	back of tongue	soft palate

Languages

Czech
Estonian
Hebrew
Navajo
Polish
Portuguese
Russian
Spanish
Urdu

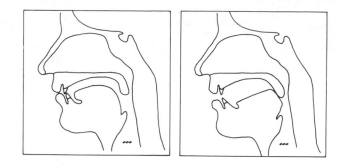

SENTENCES WITH CONTEXTUAL CLUES

(med.) He HANGS the best HAMS.
Get the HAMMER from the HANGER.

(fin.) The RING is on the RIM.
Was that SAM who SANG?
Can you BRING it to the BRIM?

MINIMAL SENTENCES

(med.) The girl is SWIMMING/SWINGING.
I heard several BOMBS/BONGS.

(fin.) He likes to HAM/HANG it up.
It was a sharp PROM/PRONG.
She had SWUM/SWUNG there for hours.

medial
bombed-bonged
clammed-clanged
bombing-bonging
clamming-clanging
dimming-dinging
slimming-slinging
rimming-ringing
brimming-bringing
swimming-swinging

slimmer-slinger
simmer-singer
swimmer-swinger
clamor-clanger
bombs-bongs
hams-hangs
clams-clangs
slims-slings
rims-rings
brims-brings

swims-swings
proms-prongs
rums-rungs

final
bomb-bong
ham-hang
clam-clang
slam-slang
ram-rang

Sam-sang
dim-ding
slim-sling
rim-ring
brim-bring
swim-swing
prom-prong
hum-hung
slum-slung
rum-rung

SOUND	VOICING	DURATION	PASSAGE	ARTICULATOR	POINT OF ARTICULATION
[p] pack	voiceless	stop	oral	lower lip	upper lip
[b] back	voiced	stop	oral	lower lip	upper lip

Languages

Arabic
Chinese
Estonian
Fijian
Finnish
German
  (final)
Hawaiian
Indonesian
  (final)
Korean
Marshallese
Micronesian
Navajo
Samoan
Spanish
Tamil
Thai
  (final)
Tongan
Turkish
Vietnamese
  (final)

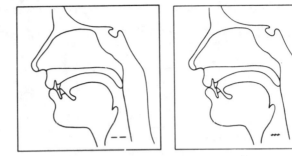

SENTENCES WITH CONTEXTUAL CLUES

(init.) The PIG is BIG.
         Please BUY a PIE.
         The PONY is rather BONY.
(med.)   Make it STABLE with a STAPLE.
(fin.)   The driver's CAP matches his CAB.

MINIMAL SENTENCES

(init.) He is going on the PIKE/BIKE.
         They POUNCED/BOUNCED on it.
         Is it in his PACK/BACK?
(med.)   They were MOPPING/MOBBING the store.
(fin.)   Put this in your LAP/LAB.

initial
pace-base
pack-back
pact-backed
pad-bad
pail-bail
pain-bane
pair-bear
palate-ballot
pale-bale
palm-balm
pan-ban
par-bar
parley-barley
paste-baste
pat-bat
patch-batch
pate-bait
path-bath
patter-batter
pay-bay
pea-bee
peach-beach
peak-beak

pear-bear
peg-beg
pelt-belt
pen-Ben
pent-bent
perch-birch
pest-best
pet-bet
pie-buy
pig-big
pike-bike
pile-bile
pill-bill
pit-bit
pitch-bitch
plank-blank
planned-bland
plaque-black
played-blade
plead-bleed
pleat-bleat
plight-blight
plot-blot
plunder-blunder

pond-bond
pole-bowl
pony-bony
pore-bore
pound-bound
poured-board
post-boast
pounce-bounce
pout-bout
pox-box
praise-braise
pray-bray
pressed-breast
prick-brick
pride-bride
prim-brim
prior-briar
puck-buck
puff-buff
pun-bun
punch-bunch
punt-bunt
purr-bur

purred-bird
pus-bus
push-bush
putter-butter

medial
stapled-stabled
rumpled-rumbled
crumpled-crumbled
dappled-dabbled
rippled-ribald
rapid-rabid
staple-stable
ample-amble
simple-symbol
crumple-crumble
rumple-rumble
dapple-dabble
nipple-nibble
stapling-stabling
crumpling-crumbling
gapping-gabbing
napping-nabbing
mopping-mobbing

sopping-sobbing
stapler-stabler
dapper-dabber
clapper-clabber

final
lope-lobe
rope-robe
cap-cab
gap-gab
lap-lab
flap-flab
slap-slab
nap-nab
tap-tab
swap-swab
rip-rib
cop-cob
lop-lob
slop-slob
mop-mob
sop-sob
sup-sub
cup-cub
pup-pub

35

SOUND	VOICING	DURATION	PASSAGE	ARTICULATOR	POINT OF ARTICULATION
[p] pat	voiceless	stop	oral	lower lip	upper lip
[f] fat	voiceless	continuant	oral	lower lip	upper teeth

Language

Arabic
Burmese
Cebuano
Georgian
Hausa
Hawaiian
Hindi
Indonesian
Javanese
Kannada
Korean
Marshallese
Navajo
Pashto
Samoan
Tagalog
Tamil
Telugu
Thai
  (final)
Tongan
Turkish
Uzbek
Vietnamese

SENTENCES WITH CONTEXTUAL CLUES

(init.)   It won't FIT in the PIT.
         He FAINTS when he PAINTS.
(med.) The PUPPY looks PUFFY.
(fin.)   The CHIEF wants it CHEAP.
         He had to LEAP to get the LEAF.

MINIMAL SENTENCES

(init.)   Did you hear about their PLIGHT/FLIGHT?
(med.) She is going to SUPPER/SUFFER.
         These are CLIPS/CLIFFS.
(fin.)   Turn your CUP/CUFF over.
         You could see the STRIPE/STRIFE.

initial
packed-fact
pad-fad
pail-fail
paint-faint
pair-fair
pan-fan
passion-fashion
past-fast
pat-fat
pays-faze
peel-feel
pickle-fickle
pig-fig
pile-file
pin-fin
pinch-finch
pit-fit
platter-flatter
plea-flea
plight-flight

plush-flush
poke-folk
pool-fool
pony-phony
pour-four
praise-phrase
prank-frank
pride-fried
prize-fries
prose-froze
pry-fry
pun-fun

medial
leaped-leafed
loped-loafed
lapped-laughed
shipped-shift
ripped-rift
sipped-sift
leaping-leafing

lapping-laughing
snipping-sniffing
cupping-cuffing
proper-proffer
copper-cougher
supper-suffer
reaps-reefs
laps-laughs
skips-skiffs
clips-cliffs
snips-sniffs
tips-tiffs
cops-coughs
cups-cuffs
pups-puffs
copy-coffee
puppy-puffy

final
stripe-strife

wipe-wife
lope-loaf
cheap-chief
leap-leaf
reap-reef
chap-chaff
beep-beef
sheep-sheaf
whip-whiff
skip-skiff
clip-cliff
snip-sniff
tip-tiff
cop-cough
hoop-hoof
gulp-gulf
limp-lymph
cup-cuff
hup-huff
pup-puff
gyp-jiff

SOUND	VOICING	DURATION	PASSAGE	ARTICULATOR	POINT OF ARTICULATION
[b] bad	voiced	stop	oral	lower lip	upper lip
[d] dad	voiced	stop	oral	tip of tongue	tooth ridge

Languages

Chinese
Estonian
Fijian
Samoan
Tongan

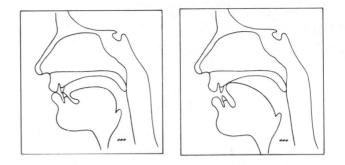

SENTENCES WITH CONTEXTUAL CLUES
(init.)   That tree's BARK is awfully DARK.
           The boy blew a BUBBLE that was DOUBLE.
           Besides being BENT, it has a DENT.
(med.)   Does the LADLE have a LABEL?
(fin.)   He TRIED to find the TRIBE.

MINIMAL SENTENCES
(init.)   Is the man BUSY/DIZZY?
           Let's BUY/DYE these curtains.
(med.)   There are some fine LABS/LADS in this school.
           It was an unusual WEBBING/WEDDING.
(fin.)   His BIB/BID was the smallest.

initial				
babble-dabble	beside-decide	bunk-dunk	webs-weds	cob-cod
bad-dad	level-devil	bust-dust	bibs-bids	gob-god
bait-date	bicker-dicker	buy-die	ribs-rids	hob-hod
bandy-dandy	big-dig		cobs-cods	knob-nod
bane-deign	bike-dike	*medial*	knobs-nods	rob-rod
bangle-dangle	bill-dill	ribald-riddled	robs-rods	sob-sod
bank-dank	bin-din	pebble-pedal	bobby-body	barb-barred
bare-dare	boat-dote	cobble-coddle	ruby-Rudy	garb-guard
bark-dark	boo-do	treble-treadle		herb-herd
barn-darn	boon-dune	webbing-wedding	*final*	curb-curd
bash-dash	bore-door	ribbing-ridding	cab-cad	blurb-blurred
bay-day	bout-doubt	label-ladle	scab-scad	cub-cud
bays-daze	brag-drag	ribbon-ridden	dab-dad	dub-dud
beacon-deacon	brain-drain	rubber-rudder	gab-gad	flub-flood
beam-deem	brawn-drawn	bribes-brides	lab-lad	stub-stud
bean-dean	bread-dread	lobes-loads	grab-grad	bribe-bride
bed-dead	brew-drew	robes-roads	squab-squad	tribe-tried
beep-deep	brink-drink	cabs-cads	deb-dead	globe-glowed
beer-deer	brown-drown	scabs-scads	web-wed	robe-road
bell-dell	bubble-double	dabs-dads	bib-bid	
bent-dent	buck-duck	gabs-gads	rib-rid	
	bump-dump	labs-lads	squib-squid	

SOUND	VOICING	DURATION	PASSAGE	ARTICULATOR	POINT OF ARTICULATION
[hw] whack	voiceless	continuant	oral	lower lip (lips are tightly rounded)	upper lip
[h] hack	voiceless	continuant	oral		

Languages

Bulgarian
Burmese
Czech
Dutch
Estonian
Fijian
Finnish
Georgian
Hebrew
Hindi
Hungarian
Javanese
Korean
Pashto
Polish
Portuguese
Russian
Samoan
Spanish
Tamil
Urdu

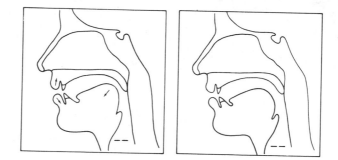

SENTENCES WITH CONTEXTUAL CLUES

(init.)   I do not know WHETHER this is HEATHER.
He hurt his HEEL on the WHEEL.
Just WHERE is his HAIR?
But WHY say HI?
WHICH shall I HITCH?

MINIMAL SENTENCES

(init.)   Is this the right WHEAT/HEAT?
The girl WHIRLED/HURLED it.
It is under his WHEEL/HEEL.
The WHALE/HAIL surprised us.
He wants WHITE/HEIGHT in the center.

initial

whack-hack
whacked-hacked
whacker-hacker
whacking-hacking
whale-hail
whaled-hailed
whaling-hailing
wham-ham
whang-hang
wheat-heat
whee-he
wheel-heel
wheeled-heeled
wheeler-healer
wheeling-healing
wheeze-he's
whelp-help
whelped-helped
whelping-helping

when-hen
whence-hence
where-hair
whether-heather
which-hitch
whim-him
whip-hip
whir-her
whirl-hurl
whirled-hurled
whirler-hurler
whirling-hurling
whist-hissed
whit-hit
white-height
whither-hither
whiz-his
whop-hop
whopping-hopping
why-hi

SOUND	VOICING	DURATION	PASSAGE	ARTICULATOR	POINT OF ARTICULATION
[w] Wac	voiced	continuant	oral	lower lip (lips are tightly rounded)	upper lip
[hw] whack	voiceless	continuant	oral	lower lip (lips are tightly rounded)	upper lip

Languages

Arabic
Burmese
Cebuano
Croatian
Czech
Danish
Dutch
Estonian
Fijian
Finnish
French
Georgian
German
Greek
Hausa
Hebrew
Hindi
Hungarian
Indonesian
Italian
Japanese
Javanese
Kannada
Korean
Marshallese
Micronesian
Norwegian
Pashto
Portuguese
Russian
Samoan
Serbian
Spanish
Swahili
Swedish
Tagalog
Tamil
Telugu
Thai
Turkish
Urdu
Uzbek
Vietnamese

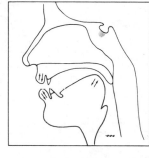 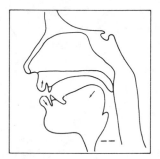

SENTENCES WITH CONTEXTUAL CLUES

(init.)   Just WHICH is a WITCH?
I WISH it wouldn't WHISH.
I don't care a WHIT about his WIT.
He heard a WHINE as he tasted the WINE.
I don't know WHETHER we'll have good WEATHER.

MINIMAL SENTENCES

(init.)   I heard a WAIL/WHALE.
It was an unusual WINE/WHINE.
Is this the WAY/WHEY?
I heard the strangest WISH/WHISH.
There are pictures of WIGS/WHIGS in the book.

initial

Wac-whack	wig-whig
wail-whale	wile-while
wailed-whaled	wind-whined
wailer-whaler	wine-whine
wailing-whaling	wining-whining
way-whey	wish-whish
wear-where	wished-whished
weather-whether	wishing-whishing
we'll-wheel	wit-whit
wet-whet	witch-which
wetting-whetting	wither-whither
wield-wheeled	Y-why

SOUND	VOICING	DURATION	PASSAGE	ARTICULATOR	POINT OF ARTICULATION
[w] west	voiced	continuant	oral	lower lip (lips are tightly rounded)	upper lip
[v] vest	voiced	continuant	oral	lower lip	upper teeth

Languages

Arabic
Bulgarian
Burmese
Chinese
Croatian
Czech
Danish
Finnish
German
Gujarati
Hausa
Hebrew
Hindi
Hungarian
Indonesian
Javanese
Norwegian
Pashto
Persian
Samoan
Serbian
Swedish
Tamil
Thai
Turkish
Urdu

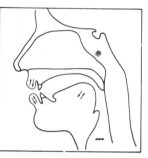 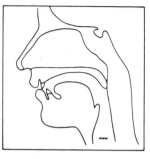

SENTENCES WITH CONTEXTUAL CLUES

(med.)   It would be WISER to clean the VISOR.
        Did WALT put it in the VAULT?
        My VERSE is getting WORSE.
(med.)   They ROVED down the ROAD.
(fin.)   Violets GROW in that GROVE.

MINIMAL SENTENCES

(init.)   That's a good WINE/VINE.
        Did you look in the WEST/VEST?
        I didn't expect to see the WIPER/VIPER.
(med.)   They ROWED/ROVED through the park.
(fin.)   The cow was MOOING/MOVING.

initial
wail-veil
Walt-vault
wane-vain
wary-vary
weird-veered
we'll-veal
wend-vend
went-vent
we're-veer
west-vest
wet-vet
wile-vile
wine-vine
wiper-viper
wiser-visor

worse-verse
wow-vow
Y-vie

medial
rowed-roved
mooing-moving
rowing-roving
rower-rover

final
dough-dove
moo-move
grew-groove
row-rove
grow-grove
stow-stove

40

SOUND	VOICING	DURATION	PASSAGE	ARTICULATOR	POINT OF ARTICULATION
[w] Wac	voiced	continuant	oral	lower lip (lips are tightly rounded)	upper lip
[r] rack	voiced	continuant	oral	tip of tongue	hard palate

Languages

Bulgarian
Burmese
Danish
Dutch
Estonian
Finnish
Hindi
Polish
Russian
Tamil
Urdu

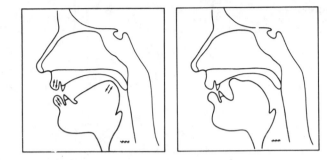

SENTENCES WITH CONTEXTUAL CLUES
(init.) Those REEDS are just WEEDS.
I will WAIT to hear the RATE.
The way he was REARED is very WEIRD.
(med.) A ROSE never ROARS.
(fin.) Can he MOW a little MORE?

MINIMAL SENTENCES
(init.) Let's go WEST/REST.
Are they WED/RED?
They just WASTE/RACED away.
(med.) They HOED/HOARD potatoes.
(fin.) They needed the DOUGH/DOOR.

initial
wad-rod
wade-raid
wag-rag
wage-rage
waist-raced
wait-rate
wake-rake
wane-rain
ware-rare
watt-rot
wave-rave
way-ray
ways-raise
wax-racks
wed-red

weed-reed
week-reek
weight-rate
weird-reared
we'll-reel
wend-rend
went-rent
west-rest
wickets-rickets
wide-ride
wife-rife
wig-rig
wild-riled
wince-rinse
wind-rind
wing-ring

wink-rink
wipe-ripe
wise-rise
witch-rich
woe-row
womb-room
won-run
wooed-rude
wound-round
medial
hoed-hoard
bowed-bored
rowed-roared
pose-pores
rose-roars
going-goring

bowing-boring
rowing-roaring
sowing-soaring
sews-sores
bows-bores
final
foe-four
toe-tore
woe-wore
dough-door
go-gore
bow-boar
low-lore
mow-more
row-roar
sow-soar

SOUND	VOICING	DURATION	PASSAGE	ARTICULATOR	POINT OF ARTICULATION
[w] wag	voiced	continuant	oral	lower lip (lips are tightly rounded)	upper lip
[g] gag	voiced	stop	oral	back of tongue	soft palate

Languages

Bulgarian
Estonian
Finnish
Greek
Hindi
Polish
Spanish
Tamil
Urdu

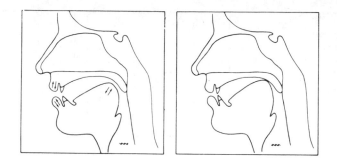

SENTENCES WITH CONTEXTUAL CLUES

(init.)   Please WAIT by the GATE.
           Don't GET all WET.
           He GAVE a big WAVE.
(med.) The COUGAR was not a COOER.
(fin.)   FEW know the FUGUE.

MINIMAL SENTENCES

(init.)   Turkeys are funny when they WOBBLE/GOBBLE.
           He gets good WAGES/GAUGES at the plant.
           Put it in the WOOD/GOOD box.
(med.) It was a little DOUGHY/DOGIE.
(fin.)   He saw the last ROW/ROGUE.

initial
wag-gag
wage-gauge
wail-gale
wait-gate
walk-gawk
wall-gall
wane-gain
warble-garble
wash-gosh
wave-gave
way-gay
ways-gaze
weird-geared
welding-gelding
west-guest
wet-get
wide-guide
wig-gig
wiggle-giggle
wile-guile

will-gill
willed-guild
wilt-guilt
wise-guise
wizard-gizzard
wobble-gobble
woe-go
won-gun
wood-good
word-gird
worth-girth

medial
reword-regird
cooer-cougar
ower-ogre
doughy-dogie

final
few-fugue
row-rogue

SOUND	VOICING	DURATION	PASSAGE	ARTICULATOR	POINT OF ARTICULATION
[f] fat	voiceless	continuant	oral	bottom lip	top teeth
[v] vat	voiced	continuant	oral	bottom lip	top teeth

Languages

Arabic
Burmese
Cebuano
Estonian
Finnish
Georgian
Hawaiian
Indonesian
Japanese
Javanese
Korean
Marshallese
Micronesian
Navajo
Pashto
Tagalog
Tamil
Thai
Vietnamese

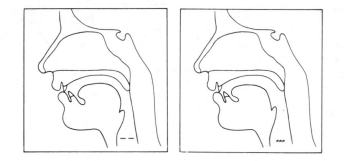

SENTENCES WITH CONTEXTUAL CLUES

(init.)   Our FAN is in the VAN.
         I don't FEEL like eating VEAL.
         Only a FEW can see this VIEW.
(med.)   His RIVAL had a RIFLE.
(fin.)   Can you SAVE enough to feel SAFE?

MINIMAL SENTENCES

(init.)   It is his FAULT/VAULT.
         They have a FAST/VAST program.
(med.)   Did he SHUFFLE/SHOVEL them?
(fin.)   I do not like to see her GRIEF/GRIEVE.
         They are beginning to LEAF/LEAVE.

---

initial
fail-veil
fairy-vary
fan-van
fast-vast
fat-vat
fault-vault
fear-veer
fee-V
feel-veal
feign-vain
fend-vend
fender-vendor
ferry-very
feud-viewed

few-view
file-vile
final-vinyl
fine-vine
first-versed
focal-vocal
foist-voiced
folly-volley
fuse-views

medial
raffled-raveled
sniffled-sniveled
shuffled-shoveled
rifled-rivaled

infested-invested
raffle-ravel
sniffle-snivel
shuffle-shovel
rifle-rival
refuse-reviews
leafing-leaving
sniffling-sniveling
shuffling-shoveling
infesting-investing
safer-saver
wafer-waiver
sniffler-sniveler
shuffler-shoveler
infest-invest

final
safe-save
fife-five
life-live
sheaf-sheave
leaf-leave
thief-thieve
belief-believe
relief-relieve
grief-grieve
waif-wave
calf-calve
half-have
proof-prove

SOUND	VOICING	DURATION	PASSAGE	ARTICULATOR	POINT OF ARTICULATION
[f] fane	voiceless	continuant	oral	bottom lip	top teeth
[θ] thane	voiceless	continuant	oral	tip of tongue	top teeth

Languages

Arabic
Burmese
Cebuano
Danish
Estonian
Finnish
Georgian
Hebrew
Hindi
Italian
Javanese
Korean
Micronesian
Navajo
Persian
Polish
Russian
Samoan
Spanish
Swedish
Tagalog
Tamil
Telugu
Tongan
Turkish
Urdu
Uzbek
Vietnamese
   (final)

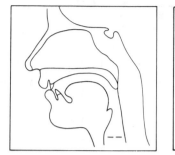
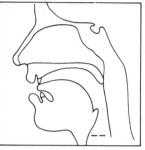

SENTENCES WITH CONTEXTUAL CLUES

(init.)   That FIN is THIN.
          FIRST let's quench our THIRST.
          If you buy THREE you get one FREE.
(med.)   Being RUTHLESS, he left them ROOFLESS.
(fin.)   Did RUTH climb on the ROOF?

MINIMAL SENTENCES

(init.)   It's an extra FRILL/THRILL for her.
          They FOUGHT/THOUGHT about it.
(med.)   He seldom LAUGHS/LATHS.
(fin.)   It is a beautiful REEF/WREATH.
          Did you hear that OAF/OATH?

initial
fie-thigh
fin-thin
fink-think
first-thirst
fought-thought
Fred-thread
free-three
fresh-thresh
fret-threat
frill-thrill
furrow-thorough

medial
laughing-lathing
refresh-rethresh
miffs-myths

laughs-laths
roofless-ruthless
refought-rethought
unfought-unthought
deafly-deathly

final
deaf-death
sheaf-sheath
oaf-oath
loaf-loth
reef-wreath
miff-myth
half-hath
roof-Ruth
laugh-lath
trough-troth

SOUND	VOICING	DURATION	PASSAGE	ARTICULATOR	POINT OF ARTICULATION
[f] fame	voiceless	continuant	oral	bottom lip	top teeth
[š] shame	voiceless	continuant	oral	front of tongue	hard palate

Languages

Burmese
Estonian
Javanese
Navajo
Tamil
Vietnamese
　(final)

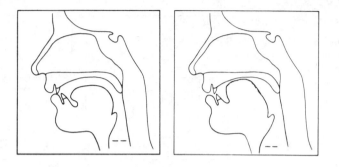

SENTENCES WITH CONTEXTUAL CLUES

(init.)　That SHINE is FINE.
　　　　Did SHE pay the FEE?
　　　　They were FED in the SHED.
(med.)　He is BLUSHING because he is BLUFFING.
(fin.)　They paid CASH for the CALF.

MINIMAL SENTENCES

(init.)　He FEARS/SHEARS sheep.
　　　　It's because of his FAME/SHAME.
(med.)　The men are ROUGHING/RUSHING it.
　　　　He LAUGHED/LASHED at it.
(fin.)　It is on a LEAF/LEASH.

initial		*medial*	
fade-shade	field-shield	leafed-leashed	daft-dashed
fag-shag	fifty-shifty	staffed-stashed	craft-crashed
fail-shale	filling-shilling	unfed-unshed	
fair-share	fin-shin	laughed-lashed	*final*
fake-shake	fine-shine	roughed-rushed	leaf-leash
fall-shawl	fire-shyer	refine-reshine	gaff-gash
fallow-shallow	foal-shoal	refute-reshoot	staff-stash
fame-shame	foe-show	leafing-leashing	whiff-whish
fatter-shatter	folder-shoulder	staffing-stashing	guff-gush
fear-shear	fort-short	whiffing-whishing	huff-hush
fed-shed	fox-shocks	fluffing-flushing	bluff-blush
fee-she	frank-shrank	roughing-rushing	fluff-flush
feel-she'll	freak-shriek	staffer-stasher	muff-mush
feet-sheet	Fred-shred	fluffer-flusher	calf-cash
fell-shell	frill-shrill	laugher-lasher	half-hash
fie-shy	fun-shun	rougher-rusher	laugh-lash
	phone-shone		rough-rush

SOUND	VOICING	DURATION	PASSAGE	ARTICULATOR	POINT OF ARTICULATION
[f] fat	voiceless	continuant	oral	bottom lip	top teeth
[s] sat	voiceless	continuant	oral	tip of tongue	tooth ridge

Languages

Burmese
Navajo
Vietnamese
    (final)

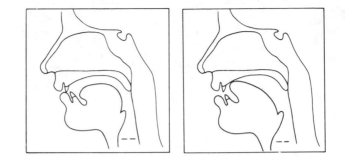

SENTENCES WITH CONTEXTUAL CLUES

(init.)   The SIGN is FINE.
          That SLAT is FLAT.
(med.)   He was MIFFED when he MISSED.
          He LAUGHED LAST.
(fin.)   Don't MUSS my MUFF.

MINIMAL SENTENCES

(init.)   He FAVORS/SAVORS it.
          This is the FITTING/SITTING room.
(med.)   It is CHAFING/CHASING the baby.
(fin.)   The LEAF/LEASE is there.
          It is on the GRAPH/GRASS.

initial
fable-sable
fact-sacked
fad-sad
fail-sail
faint-saint
fake-sake
fallow-sallow
fame-same
famine-salmon
fang-sang
fat-sat
fault-salt
favor-savor
fear-sear
feat-seat
fed-said
fee-see
feel-seal
feign-sane
fence-sense

fender-sender
fervent-servant
fickle-sickle
field-sealed
fight-sight
fill-sill
fin-sin
fine-sign
fire-sire
fist-cyst
fit-sit
fitting-sitting
fix-six
fizzle-sizzle
flag-slag
flap-slap
flash-slash
flat-slat
flax-slacks
fleet-sleet
flicker-slicker

flight-slight
fling-sling
flip-slip
flit-slit
flow-slow
flush-slush
fly-sly
foal-soul
foe-so
foil-soil
fold-sold
folk-soak
foot-soot
force-source
fort-sort
found-sound
four-sore
fox-socks
fun-sun
fur-sir
phone-sewn

medial
leafed-leased
chafed-chased
miffed-mist
buffed-bust
muffed-must
laughed-last
coughed-cost
roughed-rust
defend-descend
whiffle-whistle
confine-consign
chafing-chasing
gaffer-gasser
sifter-sister
left-lest
reft-rest
weft-west
lift-list
rift-wrist
sift-cyst

loft-lost

final
life-lice
knife-nice
rife-rice
leaf-lease
relief-release
grief-grease
gaff-gas
Jeff-Jess
miff-miss
goof-goose
buff-bus
cuff-cuss
muff-muss
puff-pus
laugh-lass
graph-grass

SOUND	VOICING	DURATION	PASSAGE	ARTICULATOR	POINT OF ARTICULATION
[f] fat	voiceless	continuant	oral	bottom lip	top teeth
[h] hat	voiceless	continuant	oral		

Languages

Burmese
Georgian
Hausa
Japanese
(before [uw] or
[u])
Javanese

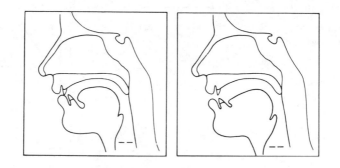

SENTENCES WITH CONTEXTUAL CLUES

(init.)   Her HAIR is FAIR.
He FOUND a HOUND.
After his FUMBLE he was HUMBLE.
I HATE my FATE.

(med.)   He was REHIRED and then REFIRED.

MINIMAL SENTENCES

(init.)   Was he hurt in the FALL/HALL?
He did not come to FARM/HARM.
The children FOUND/HOUND the man.
She was FOLDING/HOLDING clothes.

(med.)   He was UNFIT/UNHIT.

initial
fad-had
fag-hag
fail-hail
fair-hair
fall-hall
fallow-hallow
falter-halter
fang-hang
fanned-hand
farm-harm
fat-hat
fate-hate
fault-halt
faze-haze
fear-hear

feather-heather
fed-head
fee-he
feed-heed
feel-heel
fell-hell
feet-heat
fence-hence
few-hue
fight-height
fill-hill
find-hind
fire-sire
fit-hit
five-hive
fix-hicks

fizz-his
foal-hole
foam-home
folks-hoax
follow-hollow
focus-hocus
foe-hoe
folly-holly
force-horse
ford-hoard
foul-howl
found-hound
fumble-humble
funny-honey
fur-her
furl-hurl

fussy-hussy
phone-hone

medial
unfailed-unhailed
unfelled-unheld
unfurled-unhurled
unfired-unhired
referred-reheard
unfollowed-unhollowed
rephone-rehone
refire-rehire
unfeeding-unheeding
unfearing-unhearing
refeel-reheel
unfit-unhit

SOUND	VOICING	DURATION	PASSAGE	ARTICULATOR	POINT OF ARTICULATION
[v] vat	voiced	continuant	oral	bottom lip	top teeth
[b] bat	voiced	stop	oral	bottom lip	upper lip

Languages

Arabic
Burmese
Cebuano
Greek
Indonesian
Japanese
Javanese
Korean
Marshallese
Navajo
Persian
Spanish
Tagalog

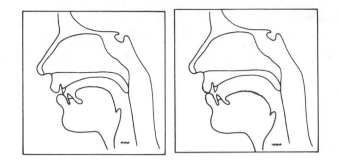

SENTENCES WITH CONTEXTUAL CLUES

(init.) This VEST is BEST.
The VENT was BENT.
Did they VOTE on the BOAT?
(med.) That MARBLE is a MARVEL.
(fin.) They are repairing the CURB on the CURVE.

MINIMAL SENTENCES

(init.) You can not VEND/BEND those here.
Use that for the VASE/BASE.
She is VYING/BUYING for the team.
(med.) I see two CALVES/CABS.
(fin.) The accident was on the CURVE/CURB.

---

initial
van-ban
vane-bane
vat-bat
veep-beep
veer-beer
veered-beard
veil-bail
vend-bend
vent-bent
very-berry
vest-best
vet-bet

vicar-bicker
vies-buys
vigor-bigger
vile-bile
virgin-burgeon
volt-bolt
vote-boat
vow-bow
vowel-bowel
vying-buying

medial
driveled-dribbled

marveled-marbled
covered-cupboard
curved-curbed
driveling-dribbling
curving-curbing
gavel-gabble
ravel-rabble
marvel-marble
drivel-dribble
lover-lubber
savor-saber
loaves-lobes
thieves-Thebes

calves-cabs
curves-curbs
prevent-prebent

final
suave-swab
jive-jibe
calve-cab
dove-dub
rove-robe
curve-curb

SOUND	VOICING	DURATION	PASSAGE	ARTICULATOR	POINT OF ARTICULATION
[v] vat	voiced	continuant	oral	bottom lip	top teeth
[ð] that	voiced	continuant	oral	tip of tongue	top teeth

Languages

Arabic
Bulgarian
Burmese
Cebuano
Czech
Danish
Dutch
Estonian
Finnish
Georgian
Hausa
Hebrew
Hindi
Italian
Javanese
Micronesian
Navajo
Persian
Polish
Russian
Swedish
Tagalog
Tamil
Urdu
Vietnamese
  (final)

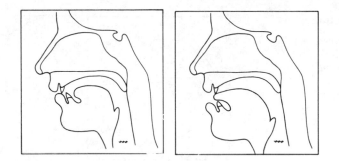

SENTENCES WITH CONTEXTUAL CLUES

(init.)   Is THAT the VAT?
          Wilt THOU repeat the VOW?
(med.) The LEATHER is near the LEVER.
          She LOATHES small LOAVES.
(fin.)   She wrote CLOTHE for CLOVE.

MINIMAL SENTENCES

(init.)   It was dipped in VAT/THAT dye.
(med.) He SHEAVED/SHEATHED it.
(fin.)   Can they REEVE/WREATHE the block?
          It was a LIVE/LITHE tree.
          Repeat the word CLOVE/CLOTHE.

initial
V-thee
van-than
vat-that
veil-they'll
vie-thy
vine-thine
vow-thou

never-nether
sliver-slither
sheaves-sheathes
loaves-loathes
reeves-wreathes
lively-lithely

medial
slivered-slithered
slivering-slithering
reeving-wreathing

final
reeve-wreathe
breve-breathe
live-lithe
clove-clothe

SOUND	VOICING	DURATION	PASSAGE	ARTICULATOR	POINT OF ARTICULATION
[v] veal	voiced	continuant	oral	bottom lip	top teeth
[z] zeal	voiced	continuant	oral	tip of tongue	tooth ridge

Languages

Burmese
Finnish
Javanese
Thai

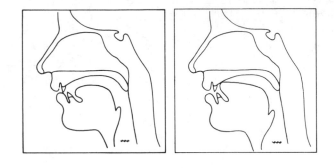

SENTENCES WITH CONTEXTUAL CLUES
(init.) He ate the VEAL with ZEAL.
(med.) A WEASEL is bigger than a WEEVIL.
(fin.) I hope it DRIES while we DRIVE.
There are many WAYS to WAVE.
What GROWS in the GROVE?

MINIMAL SENTENCES
(init.) He ate it with VEAL/ZEAL.
(med.) It is a small black RAVEN/RAISIN.
Give it to DAVY/DAISY.
(fin.) I heard the cows(') MOVE/MOOS.
When will he ARRIVE/ARISE?

initial
veal-zeal
vest-zest
veiny-zany
voom-zoom

medial
driveled-drizzled
divined-designed
raved-raised
braved-braised
craved-crazed
divine-design
raving-raising

drivel-drizzle
novel-nozzle
weevil-weasel
civil-sizzle
raven-raisin
haven't-hasn't
Davy-daisy
divvy-dizzy

final
Dave-daze
heave-he's
sheave-she's
gave-gaze
have-has

slave-slays
pave-pays
rave-rays
brave-brays
crave-craze
grave-graze
stave-stays
wave-ways
peeve-peas
I've-eyes
dive-dies
live-lies
drive-dries
arrive-arise
revive-revise

shelve-shells
dove-does
clove-close
move-moos
rove-rose
grove-grows
stove-stows
wove-woes
carve-cars
starve-stars
serve-sirs
curve-curs

SOUND	VOICING	DURATION	PASSAGE	ARTICULATOR	POINT OF ARTICULATION
[θ] thank	voiceless	continuant	oral	tip of tongue	top teeth
[t] tank	voiceless	stop	oral	tip of tongue	tooth ridge

Languages

Arabic
  (Libyan)
Bulgarian
Cebuano
Croatian
Czech
Danish
Dutch
Estonian
Georgian
German
Hawaiian
Hebrew
Hindi
Hungarian
Indonesian
Italian
Japanese
Javanese
Korean
Marshallese
Micronesian
Navajo
Norwegian
Pashto
Persian
Polish
Portuguese
Russian
Samoan
Serbian
Spanish
  (American)
Swahili
Swedish
Tagalog
Tamil
Telugu
Thai
Tongan
Turkish
Urdu
Uzbek
Vietnamese

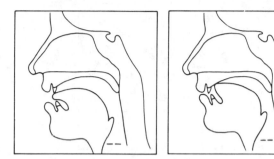

SENTENCES WITH CONTEXTUAL CLUES

(init.)   He TAUGHT what he THOUGHT.
          He said THANKS for the TANKS.
(med.)   It's a PITY they've turned PITHY.
(fin.)   The CLOTH will help it CLOT.
          She BROUGHT some BROTH.

MINIMAL SENTENCES

(init.)   That's a good THEME/TEAM.
          He THOUGHT/TAUGHT about her.
(med.)   She was sad about the DEATHS/DEBTS.
(fin.)   It's the new MATH/MAT.
          He can't stand the king's WRATH/RAT.

initial
thank-tank
thankful-tankful
theme-team
thick-tick
thicker-ticker
thicket-ticket
thigh-tie
thin-tin
thing-ting
thinker-tinker
thinner-tinner
thong-tong
Thor-tore
thorn-torn
thought-taught
thrash-trash
thread-tread
three-tree
threw-true
thrill-trill
thrust-trust

thug-tug

medial
rethread-retread
ether-eater
deaths-debts
sheaths-sheets
oaths-oats
faiths-fates
tenths-tents
fourths-forts
drouths-droughts
growths-groats
myths-mitts
bathless-batless
deathless-debtless
pithy-pity

final
bath-bat
death-debt

heath-heat
sheath-sheet
math-mat
oath-oat
path-pat
wrath-rat
swath-swat
faith-fate
pith-pit
with-wit
tenth-tent
both-boat
booth-boot
tooth-toot
broth-brought
froth-fraught
dearth-dirt
hearth-heart
forth-fort
drouth-drought
growth-groat
myth-mitt

SOUND	VOICING	DURATION	PASSAGE	ARTICULATOR	POINT OF ARTICULATION
[Θ] thank	voiceless	continuant	oral	tip of tongue	top teeth
[š] shank	voiceless	continuant	oral	front of tongue	hard palate

Languages

Arabic
Bulgarian
Cebuano
Dutch
Estonian
Georgian
Hebrew
Hindi
Indonesian
Italian
Japanese
Javanese
Korean
Micronesian
Navajo
Persian
Samoan
Spanish
Tagalog
Tamil
Tongan
Urdu
Vietnamese

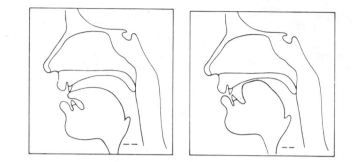

SENTENCES WITH CONTEXTUAL CLUES

(init.) The THIEF took a SHEAF.
 The SHREW is THROUGH.
(med.) He's RETHREADING the RESHREDDING machine.
(fin.) The WELSH have great WEALTH.
 She is HARSH if ashes are on the HEARTH.

MINIMAL SENTENCES

(init.) Her coat was in THREADS/SHREDS.
(med.) The workers are LATHING/LASHING the boat.
(fin.) The boy suffered from his WRATH/RASH.
 She gave him a BATH/BASH.
 He brought in the LATH/LASH.

initial
thank-shank
thanked-shanked
thankless-shankless
thaw-pshaw
thief-sheaf
thieves-sheaves
thigh-shy
thin-shin
thinned-shinned
Thor-shore
thorn-shorn
thread-shred
threaded-shredded
threading-shredding
thrill-shrill
thrilled-shrilled
thriller-shriller
thrive-shrive

through-shrew

medial
rethread-reshred
rethreaded-reshredded
unthanked-unshanked
rethreading-reshredding
lathing-lashing

final
bath-bash
hath-hash
lath-lash
math-mash
wrath-rash
with-wish
wealth-Welsh
froth-frosh
hearth-harsh

SOUND	VOICING	DURATION	PASSAGE	ARTICULATOR	POINT OF ARTICULATION
[θ] thank	voiceless	continuant	oral	tip of tongue	top teeth
[s] sank	voiceless	continuant	oral	tip of tongue	tooth ridge

Languages

Arabic
Bulgarian
Cebuano
Chinese
Danish
Dutch
Estonian
Finnish
French
Georgian
German
Hausa
Hawaiian
Hebrew
Hindi
Hungarian
Indonesian
Italian
Japanese
Javanese
Korean
Micronesian
Navajo
Persian
Polish
Russian
Samoan
Spanish
  (American)
Swedish
Tagalog
Tamil
Tongan
Urdu
Vietnamese

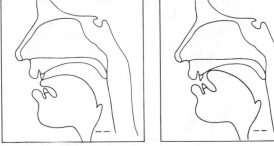

SENTENCES WITH CONTEXTUAL CLUES

(init.) Being THIN is no SIN.
         We SAW the THAW.
         I don't THINK it will SINK.
(med.)   Besides being MOSSY it is all MOTHY.
(fin.)   Their GROSS shows a steady GROWTH.

MINIMAL SENTENCES

(init.) I never THOUGHT/SOUGHT it.
         The sailors can't THINK/SINK that.
(med.)   That child is sort of MOUTHY/MOUSY.
(fin.)   They went over the PATH/PASS.
         He is the TENTH/TENSE child.

initial		*medial*	*final*
thank-sank	thin-sin	unthawed-unsawed	bath-bass
thaw-saw	thing-sing	unthinkable-unsinkable	lath-lass
thawed-sawed	think-sink	unthinking-unsinking	math-mass
thawing-sawing	thinker-sinker	rethink-resink	path-pass
theme-seem	thinking-sinking	faithless-faceless	Beth-Bess
thick-sick	thinned-sinned	truthless-truceless	faith-face
thicken-sicken	thinner-sinner	mouthiness-mousiness	kith-kiss
thickening-sickening	thinning-sinning	unthought-unsought	tenth-tense
thicker-sicker	Thor-sore	mothy-mossy	moth-moss
thickest-sickest	thought-sought	mouthy-mousy	forth-force
thigh-sigh	thuds-suds	tenthly-tensely	worth-worse
thimble-symbol	thumb-some		mouth-mouse
	thump-sump		

SOUND	VOICING	DURATION	PASSAGE	ARTICULATOR	POINT OF ARTICULATION
[ð] thy	voiced	continuant	oral	tip of tongue	top teeth
[θ] thigh	voiceless	continuant	oral	tip of tongue	top teeth

Languages

Arabic
Bulgarian
Cebuano
Chinese
Czech
Dutch
Estonian
Fijian
Finnish
French
Georgian
German
Hawaiian
Hebrew
Hindi
Hungarian
Indonesian
Italian
Japanese
Javanese
Korean
Micronesian
Navajo
Persian
Polish
Portuguese
Russian
Samoan
Spanish
Swahili
Swedish
Tagalog
Tamil
Telugu
Thai
Tongan
Turkish
Urdu
Uzbek
Vietnamese

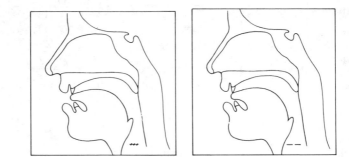

SENTENCES WITH CONTEXTUAL CLUES

(med.) He will EITHER get ETHER or novocain.
(fin.) Please SHEATHE it in a SHEATH.
        The baby's TEETH will soon TEETHE.
        They will WREATHE him in a WREATH.
        I am LOTH to LOATHE anyone.

MINIMAL SENTENCES

(init.) He can spell THY/THIGH.
(med.)   I don't like EITHER/ETHER.
         He makes a good LATHER/LATHER.
(fin.)   Say the word LOATHE/LOTH.
         They will SHEATHE/SHEATH the blade.

initial
this'll-thistle
thy-thigh

medial
either-ether

final
sheathe-sheath
wreathe-wreath
loathe-loth
teethe-teeth
mouth-mouth

SOUND	VOICING	DURATION	PASSAGE	ARTICULATOR	POINT OF ARTICULATION
[ð] than	voiced	continuant	oral	tip of tongue	top teeth
[d] Dan	voiced	stop	oral	tip of tongue	tooth ridge

Languages

Arabic
  (Libyan)
Bulgarian
Cebuano
Chinese
Croatian
Czech
Danish
Dutch
Estonian
Fijian
Georgian
German
Hawiian
Hebrew
Hungarian
Indonesian
Italian
Japanese
Javanese
Korean
Marshallese
Micronesian
Navajo
Norwegian
Pashto
Persian
Polish
Russian
Samoan
Serbian
Spanish
Swahili
Swedish
Tagalog
Thai
Tongan
Turkish
Urdu
Vietnamese

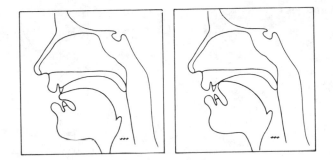

SENTENCES WITH CONTEXTUAL CLUES

(init.) I don't DARE go THERE.
  Are THOSE the men who DOZE?
  By THEN he'll be in the DEN.
(med.) He LOATHES carrying big LOADS.
(fin.) How does this BREED manage to BREATHE?

MINIMAL SENTENCES

(init.) When will THEY/DAY come?
  It's forbidden to THOSE/DOZE in class.
(med.) That teacher LOATHES/LOADS his students.
(fin.) They SOOTH/SUED him.
  Rabbits BREATHE/BREED quickly.

initial
than-Dan
their-dare
then-den
thence-dense
they-day
thine-dine
those-doze
though-dough
thy-die

medial
breathing-breeding
wreathing-reading
loathing-loading
seething-seeding
writhing-riding
breather-breeder
wreather-reader
father-fodder
lather-ladder
writher-rider

other-udder
worthier-wordier
breathes-breeds
loathes-loads
worthiness-wordiness
worthily-wordily
worthy-wordy

final
bathe-bayed
sheathe-she'd
breathe-breed
wreathe-reed
lathe-laid
loathe-load
seethe-seed
teethe-teed
writhe-ride
tithe-tide
soothe-sued
scythe-side

SOUND	VOICING	DURATION	PASSAGE	ARTICULATOR	POINT OF ARTICULATION
[ð] then	voiced	continuant	oral	tip of tongue	top teeth
[z] Zen	voiced	continuant	oral	tip of tongue	tooth ridge

Languages

Arabic
Bulgarian
Cebuano
Chinese
Czech
Danish
Dutch
Estonian
Fijian
French
Georgian
German
Greek
Hausa
Hawaiian
Hebrew
Hindi
Hungarian
Indonesian
Italian
Japanese
Javanese
Korean
Micronesian
Navajo
Polish
Russian
Samoan
Spanish
Swedish
Tagalog
Tamil
Thai
Tongan
Urdu
Vietnamese

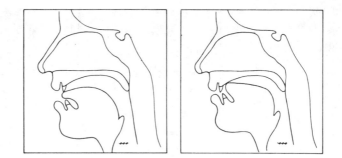

SENTENCES WITH CONTEXTUAL CLUES

(init.) It was THEN that they studied ZEN.
(med.) Stop TEASING while she's TEETHING.
(fin.) He LAYS it on the LATHE.
Can you BATHE in both BAYS?
BREATHE the fresh BREEZE.
Please SOOTH that friend of SUE'S.

MINIMAL SENTENCES

(med.) Is it CLOTHING/CLOSING?
The baby is TEETHING/TEASING.
(fin.) She gave him the LATHE/LEIS.
He is beginning to WRITHE/RISE.
The bishop asked for his TITHE/TIES.

initial
thee-Z
then-Zen
thither-zither

teether-teaser
writher-riser

medial
breathed-breezed
lathed-lazed
seethed-seized
teethed-teased
clothed-closed
breathing-breezing
seething-seizing
teething-teasing
writhing-rising
clothing-closing
seether-seizer

final
bathe-bays
sheathe-she's
breathe-breeze
lathe-lays
loathe-lows
seethe-seize
teethe-tease
writhe-rise
tithe-ties
clothe-close
soothe-sues
scythe-size

SOUND	VOICING	DURATION	PASSAGE	ARTICULATOR	POINT OF ARTICULATION
[n] knack	voiced	continuant	nasal	tip of tongue	tooth ridge
[l] lack	voiced	continuant	oral	tip of tongue (air flows around sides of tongue)	tooth ridge

Languages

Chinese
Estonian
Thai
   (final)
Vietnamese
   (final)

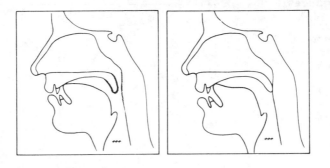

SENTENCES WITH CONTEXTUAL CLUES

(init.)   It is NOT a LOT.
           You NEED to LEAD.
           My NIECE has the LEASE.
(med.)   It was the HOUND that HOWLED.
(fin.)   Have you SEEN a SEAL?

MINIMAL SENTENCES

(init.)   It is on the NINE/LINE.
           What kind of NUMBER/LUMBER is that?
(med.)   He is WINNING/WILLING.
(fin.)   Bring me the SPOON/SPOOL.
           He traveled on the TRAIN/TRAIL.

initial
gnash-lash
gnaw-law
gnome-loam
knack-lack
knee-lee
knit-lit
knock-lock
known-loan
nag-lag
name-lame
nap-lap
near-leer
need-lead
neighbor-labor
nest-lest
net-let
never-lever
nice-lice
nick-lick
niece-lease

nigh-lie
night-light
nine-line
nip-lip
no-low
node-load
nook-look
noon-loon
noose-loose
not-lot
notice-lotus
notion-lotion
nude-lewd
null-lull
number-lumber
nymph-lymph

medial
snob-slob
found-fouled
hound-howled

ground-growled
snide-slide
minute-millet
snag-slag
leavening-leveling
feigning-failing
raining-railing
coining-coiling
chinning-chilling
winning-willing
snug-slug
snack-slack
sneek-sleek
snap-slap
crooner-crueler
snicker-slicker
tenor-teller
dens-dells
battens-battles
bins-bills
coins-coils

pins-pills
dons-dolls
fawns-falls
meany-mealy
snow-slow

final
sane-sail
wane-wail
dine-dial
fine-file
mine-mile
pine-pile
tine-tile
bone-bowl
condone-condole
phone-foal
drone-droll
tone-toll
dean-deal
mean-meal

moan-mole
roan-roll
Ben-bell
den-dell
keen-keel
seen-seal
teen-teal
hen-hell
ten-tell
even-evil
yen-yell
feign-fail
in-ill
gain-gale
main-mail
fin-fill
chin-chill
don-doll
spoon-spool
earn-earl
known-knoll

SOUND	VOICING	DURATION	PASSAGE	ARTICULATOR	POINT OF ARTICULATION
[n] fan	voiced	continuant	nasal	tip of tongue	tooth ridge
[ŋ] fang	voiced	continuant	nasal	back of tongue	soft palate

Languages

Arabic
Bulgarian
Chinese
Croatian
Czech
Estonian
French
Georgian
Greek
Hausa
Hawaiian
Hebrew
Hungarian
Italian
Japanese
Navajo
Persian
Polish
Portuguese
Russian
Samoan
Serbian
Spanish
Telugu
Turkish
Urdu

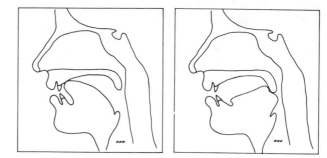

SENTENCES WITH CONTEXTUAL CLUES

(med.)   Tomorrow he WINS his WINGS.
(fin.)   The GONG is GONE.
        The CLAN heard the CLANG.
        The KING is our KIN.
        That THING is THIN.

MINIMAL SENTENCES

(med.)   He is a SINNER/SINGER.
        FANS/FANGS can be dangerous.
(fin.)   That's pretty LAWN/LONG.
        He is our KIN/KING.
        We knew it was RON/WRONG.

medial	*final*
banned-banged	done-dung
fanned-fanged	gone-gong
pinned-pinged	ban-bang
hand-hanged	fan-fang
wind-winged	clan-clang
banning-banging	ran-rang
pinning-pinging	tan-tang
sinning-singing	bin-bing
winning-winging	din-ding
banner-banger	thin-thing
sinner-singer	kin-king
bans-bangs	pin-ping
fans-fangs	sin-sing
bins-bings	win-wing
thins-things	ton-tongue
wins-wings	run-rung
tons-tongues	sun-sung
runs-rungs	stun-stung
winless-wingless	lawn-long

SOUND	VOICING	DURATION	PASSAGE	ARTICULATOR	POINT OF ARTICULATION
[t] tack	voiceless	stop	oral	tip of tongue	tooth ridge
[p] pack	voiceless	stop	oral	lower lip	upper lip

Languages

Arabic
Hindi

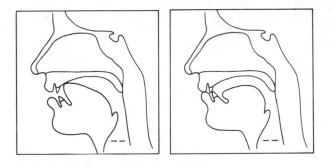

SENTENCES WITH CONTEXTUAL CLUES

(init.)   Put the TILE in the PILE.
(med.)   They were SITTING and SIPPING.
(fin.)   My PET has no PEP.
        I think it is CHEAP to CHEAT.
        It will taste RIGHT when it is RIPE.

MINIMAL SENTENCES

(init.)   The model was TRIM/PRIM.
        That's my favorite TIE/PIE.
(med.)   He was a PETTY/PEPPY thief.
        What did the LETTER/LEPER say?
(fin.)   It was a long SHOT/SHOP.

initial
tack-pack
tact-packed
tail-pail
taint-paint
tamper-pamper
tan-pan
tang-pang
taper-paper
tar-par
tart-part
taste-paste
tea-pea
teach-peach
teak-peak
tear-pair
tear-peer
tease-peas
ten-pen
tenant-pennant
tending-pending
tension-pension
tent-pent

terse-purse
test-pest
ticket-picket
tickle-pickle
tie-pie
tiled-piled
till-pill
tin-pin
tire-pyre
toast-post
told-polled
toll-poll
ton-pun
tool-pool
top-pop
tough-puff
tour-poor
tower-power
trade-prayed
tray-pray
trays-praise
tresses-presses
trick-prick

trim-prim
try-pry
tuck-puck
type-pipe

medial
beating-beeping
heating-heaping
coating-coping
looting-looping
chatting-chapping
matting-mapping
slitting-slipping
sitting-sipping
cater-caper
cheater-cheaper
sweeter-sweeper
helter-helper
clatter-clapper
flatter-flapper
letter-leper
skitter-skipper
flitter-flipper

hotter-hopper
totter-topper
utter-upper
suitor-super
grates-grapes
hatless-hapless
cats-caps
heats-heaps
petty-peppy
putty-puppy

final
ate-ape
gate-gape
trite-tripe
dote-dope
cat-cap
heat-heap
cheat-cheap
peat-peep
great-grape
seat-seep

flat-flap
slat-slap
mat-map
coat-cope
pat-pap
rat-rap
sat-sap
beet-beep
sheet-sheep
sleet-sleep
sweet-sweep
pet-pep
right-ripe
skit-skip
slit-slip
grit-grip
writ-rip
hot-hop
shot-shop
plot-plop
loot-loop
putt-pup
cut-cup

SOUND	VOICING	DURATION	PASSAGE	ARTICULATOR	POINT OF ARTICULATION
[t] tab	voiceless	stop	oral	tip of tongue	tooth ridge
[d] dab	voiced	stop	oral	tip of tongue	tooth ridge

Languages

Arabic
  (final)
Dutch
  (final)
Estonian
Finnish
German
  (final)
Hawaiian
Indonesian
  (final)
Italian
Korean
Marshallese
Micronesian
Persian
Tamil
Thai
  (final)
Vietnamese
  (final)

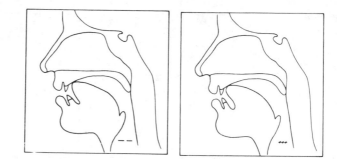

SENTENCES WITH CONTEXTUAL CLUES

(init.) Just DIP the TIP.
          I will TRY to make it DRY.
(med.) She was PATTING the PADDING.
(fin.)   I can't WAIT to WADE.
          Will she SEND one CENT?

MINIMAL SENTENCES

(init.) He seemed a little TENSE/DENSE.
          Do you have the TIME/DIME?
(med.) He is HURTING/HERDING the sheep.
          He was a TRAITOR/TRADER to England.
(fin.)   They burned the CART/CARD.

initial
tab-dab
tale-dale
tally-dally
tame-dame
tamp-damp
tamper-damper
tangle-dangle
tank-dank
tart-dart
taunt-daunt
teal-deal
team-deem
tear-dear
tear-dare
teen-dean
tell-dell
ten-den
tense-dense
tent-dent
tick-Dick
tide-died
tie-die

tike-dike
tile-dial
till-dill
time-dime
tin-din
tint-dint
tip-dip
to-do
toe-doe
tomb-doom
tome-dome
ton-done
tore-door
tot-dot
touch-Dutch
town-down
tower-dour
train-drain
traipse-drapes
tread-dread
trench-drench
tried-dried
trill-drill

trip-drip
troop-droop
true-drew
trunk-drunk
try-dry
tuck-duck
tune-dune
tusk-dusk

medial
title-tidal
heating-heeding
bleating-bleeding
pleating-pleading
seating-seeding
coating-coding
rating-raiding
slighting-sliding
sighting-siding
molting-molding
scenting-sending
hurting-herding
patting-padding

betting-bedding
plotting-plodding
putting-pudding
eaten-Eden
sweeten-Sweden
neater-kneader
renter-render
garter-guarder
latter-ladder
bitter-bidder
utter-udder
shutter-shudder
traitor-trader
catty-caddy

final
spite-spied
at-add
bat-bad
cat-cad
heat-heed
bleat-bleed
pleat-plead

meat-mead
neat-need
threat-thread
seat-seed
fat-fad
hat-had
oat-ode
coat-code
goat-goad
moat-mode
pat-pad
brat-brad
sat-sad
debt-dead
bet-bed
beet-bead
let-led
bright-bride
hit-hid
built-build
plant-planned
cot-cod
cart-card
lout-loud

SOUND	VOICING	DURATION	PASSAGE	ARTICULATOR	POINT OF ARTICULATION
[t] tap	voiceless	stop	oral	tip of tongue	tooth ridge
[č] chap	voiceless	affricate	oral	front of tongue	hard palate

Languages

Fijian
Hawaiian
Indonesian
Portuguese
Samoan
Tongan

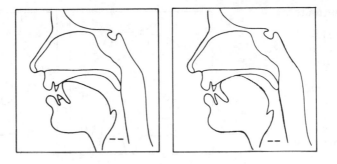

SENTENCES WITH CONTEXTUAL CLUES

(init.) Its TIP has a CHIP.
       You're in TIME to hear it CHIME.
(med.) She is MATCHING the MATTING.
(fin.) They EACH will EAT.
       The BENCH is BENT.

MINIMAL SENTENCES

(init.) He TALKED/CHALKED it up.
       She is PATTING/PATCHING it.
(med.) He is PUNTING/PUNCHING the ball.
(fin.) They are going on a HUNT/HUNCH.
       Can you RENT/WRENCH it from him?

initial
talk-chalk
tamp-champ
tap-chap
tar-char
tart-chart
tarter-charter
taste-chased
teak-cheek
tear-chair
tear-cheer
tease-cheese
test-chest
tick-chick
tide-chide
tiled-child
till-chill
time-chime
tin-chin
tip-chip
tock-chock
toes-chose

top-chop
tore-chore
tuck-chuck
turn-churn
two-chew
twos-choose

medial
bleating-bleaching
coating-coaching
belting-belching
ranting-ranching
renting-wrenching
squinting-squinching
hunting-hunching
punting-punching
parting-parching
starting-starching
batting-batching
matting-matching
patting-patching
hitting-hitching

pitting-pitching
blotting-blotching
teeter-teacher
matter-matcher
patter-patcher
twitter-twitcher
martyr-marcher
witty-witchy

final
rote-roach
bat-batch
cat-catch
eat-each
beat-beach
peat-peach
bleat-bleach
hat-hatch
mat-match
coat-coach
pat-patch
it-itch

hit-hitch
whit-which
pit-pitch
wit-witch
belt-belch
rant-ranch
bent-bench
rent-wrench
flint-flinch
bunt-bunch
hunt-hunch
punt-punch
blot-blotch
art-arch
mart-march
part-parch
start-starch
pert-perch
port-porch
mutt-much
hut-hutch
out-ouch

61

SOUND	VOICING	DURATION	PASSAGE	ARTICULATOR	POINT OF ARTICULATION
[d] dash	voiced	stop	oral	tip of tongue	tooth ridge
[r] rash	voiced	continuant	oral	tip of tongue	hard palate

Languages

Burmese
Cebuano
Croatian
Dutch
Estonian
Korean
Navajo
Serbian
Tagalog

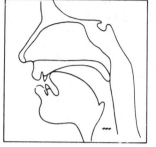 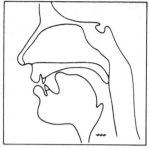

SENTENCES WITH CONTEXTUAL CLUES

(init.) It is DIM on the RIM.
The RAMP is DAMP.
(med.) Get a CADDY to CARRY.
(fin.) It was STOWED in the STORE.
He was LED to the LAIR.

MINIMAL SENTENCES

(init.) They will DEVISE/REVISE the plan.
Did they DENT/RENT it?
Is it a DEAL/REEL?
(med.) He HIDES/HIRES criminals.
(fin.) Has the TIDE/TIRE come in?

initial
dam-ram
damp-ramp
Dane-rain
danger-ranger
dangle-wrangle
dare-rare
dash-rash
date-rate
day-ray
daze-raise
dead-red
deal-reel
dear-rear
deceit-receipt
deceive-receive
decent-recent
deception-reception
deck-wreck
decline-recline
deduce-reduce
deed-reed
deem-ream

deep-reap
defer-refer
define-refine
deflect-reflect
deform-reform
dejected-rejected
dent-rent
depress-repress
deserve-reserve
design-resign
detail-retail
detain-retain
detract-retract
devise-revise
did-rid
diet-riot
dim-rim
dime-rhyme
dip-rip
dissolve-resolve
ditch-rich
division-revision
dock-rock

dole-role
done-run
doom-room
door-roar
dope-rope
dot-rot
doubt-rout
dub-rub
due-rue
dude-rude
dumb-rum
dump-rump
dust-rust
dye-rye

medial
undeformed-unreformed
undesigned-unresigned
undated-unrated
undented-unrented
undeceived-unreceived
undazed-unraised
goading-goring

hiding-hiring
siding-siring
coding-coring
redeal-rereel
hides-hires
odes-oars
codes-cores
roads-roars
caddy-carry

final
head-hair
goad-gore
load-lore
road-roar
toad-tore
bed-bear
died-dire
hid-hear
cod-car
code-core

SOUND	VOICING	DURATION	PASSAGE	ARTICULATOR	POINT OF ARTICULATION
[d] dipper	voiced	stop	oral	tip of tongue	tooth ridge
[z] zipper	voiced	continuant	oral	tip of tongue	tooth ridge

Languages

Dutch
Estonian
Finnish
Hawaiian
Japanese
  (before [uw] or
  [u])
Javanese
Korean

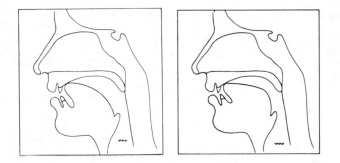

SENTENCES WITH CONTEXTUAL CLUES

(init.)   What will they DO at the ZOO?
(med.) That LADY is LAZY.
         They are SIZING the SIDING.
(fin.)   He MADE a MAZE.
         There are ROWS by the ROAD.

MINIMAL SENTENCES

(init.)   That's my DIPPER/ZIPPER.
(med.) She stepped over the PUDDLE/PUZZLE.
         She was PLEADING/PLEASING.
(fin.)   That's a southern BREED/BREEZE.
         What SLOWED/SLOWS him down?

initial
deal-zeal
don Zen
deuce-Zeus
dig-zig
ding-zing
dip-zip
dipped-zipped
dipper-zipper
dipping-zipping
dither-zither
do-zoo
doom-zoom
doomed-zoomed
dooming-zooming

medial
fiddle-fizzle
griddle-grizzle
muddle-muzzle
pleading-pleasing
fading-fazing
blading-blazing

grading-grazing
budding-buzzing
breeding-breezing
raiding-raising
riding-rising
siding-sizing
brooding-bruising
ridden-risen
hadn't-hasn't
lady-lazy
gaudy-gauzy

final
bead-bees
plead-please
knead-knees
had-has
goad-goes
road-rows
toad-toes
feed-fees
breed-breeze
decreed-decrees

freed-freeze
agreed-agrees
seed-sees
weighed-ways
lied-lies
spied-spies
cried-cries
fried-fries
tried-tries
tied-ties
hoed-hose
flavored-flavors
cued-cues
glued-glues
clawed-claws
sewed-sews
showed-shows
flowed-flows
glowed-glows
slowed-slows
snowed-snows
bayed-bays
played-plays

displayed-displays
brayed-brays
prayed-prays
stayed-stays
dyed-dies
laid-lays
paid-pays
raid-raise
hid-his
brood-bruise
dud-does
feud-fuse
lewd-lose
shrewd-shrews
fade-phase
blade-blaze
glade-glaze
made-maze
grade-graze
trade-trays
bide-buys
ride-rise
crude-cruise

SOUND	VOICING	DURATION	PASSAGE	ARTICULATOR	POINT OF ARTICULATION
[d] dab	voiced	stop	oral	tip of tongue	tooth ridge
[j] jab	voiced	affricate	oral	front of tongue	hard palate

Languages

Arabic
Estonian
Fijian
Finnish
Hawaiian
Indonesian
Japanese
  (before [iy] or [i])
Portuguese
Samoan
Tongan

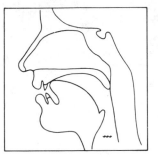 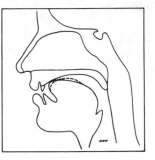

SENTENCES' WITH CONTEXTUAL CLUES

(init.)   The JEEP is in DEEP.
         We have a DEBT on the JET.
         The DEANS will not allow JEANS.
(med.)   They are AIDING the AGING.
(fin.)   Has he PAID for this PAGE?

MINIMAL SENTENCES

(init.)   Can he DUMP/JUMP it?
         Won't that DAM/JAM it up?
(med.)   Did you hear about the MURDER/MERGER?
         The Indians were RAIDING/RAGING.
(fin.)   It will AID/AGE them.

initial
dab-jab
dabber-jabber
dale-jail
dam-jam
Dane-Jane
daunt-jaunt
day-jay
deans-jeans
debt-jet
deep-jeep
deer-jeer
dig-jig
digger-jigger
dim-gym
dive-jive
doe-Joe
dolly-jolly
doused-joust
duke-juke

dump-jump
dune-June
dunk-junk
dust-just

medial
addenda-agenda
cuddle-cudgel
heading-hedging
dreading-dredging
wading-waging
sledding-sledging
wedding-wedging
budding-budging
seeding-sieging
aiding-aging
raiding-raging
fording-forging
wader-wager

raider-rager
larder-larger
murder-merger
eddy-edgy

final
bad-badge
head-hedge
dread-dredge
added-adage
banded-bandage
seed-siege
carried-carriage
married-marriage
curried-courage
billed-bilge
sled-sledge
arraigned-arrange
chained-change

rained-range
strained-strange
sinned-singe
barred-barge
charred-charge
purred-purge
footed-footage
wed-wedge
hewed-huge
stayed-stage
aid-age
paid-page
raid-rage
rid-ridge
languid-language
build-bilge
lard-large
ford-forge
bud-budge
wade-wage

SOUND	VOICING	DURATION	PASSAGE	ARTICULATOR	POINT OF ARTICULATION
[l] lack	voiced	continuant	oral	tip of tongue (air flows around sides of tongue)	tooth ridge
[r] rack	voiced	continuant	oral	tip of tongue	hard palate

Languages

Burmese
Chinese
Dutch
Hawaiian
Japanese
Korean
Micronesian
Samoan
Swahili
Thai
  (initial)
Vietnamese

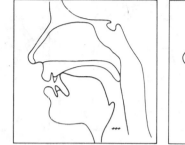
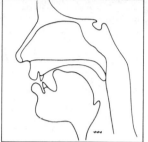

SENTENCES WITH CONTEXTUAL CLUES

(init.) There is a LIGHT on the RIGHT.
  They were LATE in announcing the RATE.
(med.) BOWLING is BORING.
  Are they FREE to FLEE?
(fin.) Here is the BILL for the BEER.

MINIMAL SENTENCES

(init.) This isn't a good LIME/RHYME.
  It is a high LOAD/ROAD.
(med.) COLLECT/CORRECT the papers.
  It is blue GLASS/GRASS.
(fin.) It was lost in the FILE/FIRE.

initial				*final*
lace-race	loaf-reef	loot-root	clutch-crutch	file-fire
lack-rack	leak-reek	lot-rot	clash-crash	mile-mire
lag-rag	leap-reap	low-row	gleen-green	tile-tire
laid-raid	leer-rear	loyal-royal	clown-crown	mole-more
lain-rain	legion-region	lug-rug	clamp-cramp	role-roar
lair-rare	lie-rye	lump-rump	miller-mirror	stole-store
lake-rake	lied-ride	lung-rung	glimmer-grimmer	dial-dire
lamb-ram	lift-rift	lush-rush	fleas-freeze	coal-core
lamp-ramp	light-right	lust-rust	files-fires	foal-four
lane-rain	limb-rim		miles-mires	goal-gore
lap-rap	lime-rhyme	*medial*	coals-cores	wall-war
lash-rash	link-rink	climb-crime	mortals-mortars	bill-beer
late-rate	lip-rip	clipped-crypt	hills-hears	dill-deer
lath-wrath	list-wrist	belated-berated	glass-grass	
laughter-rafter	liver-river	believed-bereaved	elect-erect	
lavish-ravish	load-road	cloud-crowd	collect-correct	
law-raw	loam-roam	flee-free	glow-grow	
lay-ray	lock-rock	clue-crew	fly-fry	
laze-rays	locker-rocker	filing-firing	belly-berry	
lead-read	long-wrong	rolling-roaring	jelly-Jerry	
	loom-room	bowling-boring	ply-pry	

65

SOUND	VOICING	DURATION	PASSAGE	ARTICULATOR	POINT OF ARTICULATION
[s] sack	voiceless	continuant	oral	tip of tongue	tooth ridge
[š] shack	voiceless	continuant	oral	front of tongue	hard palate

Languages

Cebuano
Estonian
Fijian
Finnish
Greek
Hawaiian
Indonesian
Japanese
  (before [iy] or [i])
Javanese
Korean
  (before [i])
Marshallese
Micronesian
Samoan
Spanish
Tagalog
Tamil
Tongan
Vietnamese

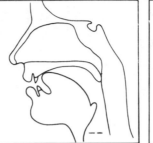 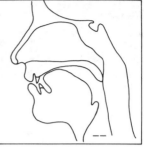

SENTENCES WITH CONTEXTUAL CLUES

(init.) Put the SACK in the SHACK.
  This SHOE fits SUE.
  Put a SHEET on the SEAT.
(med.) That is the LAST to be LASHED.
(fin.) He belongs to a PARISH in PARIS.

MINIMAL SENTENCES

(init.) Can you take a SIP/SHIP?
  SEW/SHOW the clothes.
  Mary SELLS/SHELLS peas.
(med.) How many CLASSES/CLASHES have they had?
(fin.) They have it on a LEASE/LEASH.

initial			
sack-shack	sell-shell	suck-shuck	classes-clashes
sag-shag	sewn-shone	sue-shoe	masses-mashes
said-shed	side-shied	suit-shoot	last-lashed
sail-shale	sift-shift	sun-shun	pussy-pushy
sake-shake	sigh-shy		
sallow-shallow	sign-shine	*medial*	*final*
Sam-sham	simmer-shimmer	leased-leashed	lease-leash
same-shame	sin-shin	gassed-gashed	gas-gash
sank-shank	single-shingle	classed-clashed	Paris-parish
save-shave	sip-ship	massed-mashed	iris-Irish
sealed-shield	sir-shirr	messed-meshed	bass-bash
seat-sheet	so-show	leasing-leashing	lass-lash
see-she	sock-shock	gassing-gashing	class-clash
seed-she'd	sop-shop	classing-clashing	mass-mash
seek-sheik	sore-shore	massing-mashing	brass-brash
seen-sheen	sort-short	messing-meshing	crass-crash
seep-sheep	sot-shot	fasten-fashion	mess-mesh
seer-sheer	soul-shoal	gasser-gasher	Swiss-swish
self-shelf	sour-shower	messer-mesher	muss-mush
	subtle-shuttle	leases-leashes	plus-plush

SOUND	VOICING	DURATION	PASSAGE	ARTICULATOR	POINT OF ARTICULATION
[s] seal	voiceless	continuant	oral	tip of tongue	tooth ridge
[z] zeal	voiced	continuant	oral	tip of tongue	tooth ridge

Languages

Arabic
Cebuano
Chinese
Danish
Estonian
Fijian
Finnish
German
Greek
Hawaiian
Indonesian
Italian
Javanese
Korean
Marshallese
Micronesian
Norwegian
Samoan
Spanish
Swedish
Tagalog
Tamil
Tongan
Vietnamese
(medial and final)

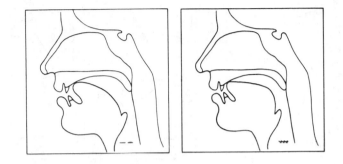

SENTENCES WITH CONTEXTUAL CLUES

(init.) I will SUE the ZOO.
There is ZINC in the SINK.
(med.) She will be FUSSY if it's FUZZY.
(fin.) The PLAYS are in this PLACE.
It PAYS to keep a fast PACE.

MINIMAL SENTENCES

(init.) She is SIPPING/ZIPPING it.
(med.) They are RACING/RAISING horses.
I heard several BUSSES/BUZZES.
He looked at her ICE/EYES.
(fin.) They did not FACE/FAZE him.

initial
seal-zeal
see-zee
seek-Zeke
sewn-zone
sing-zing
singer-zinger
singing-zinging
sink-zinc
sip-zip
sipped-zipped
sipper-zipper
sipping-zipping
sounds-zounds
sue-zoo

medial
muscle-muzzle

gristle-grizzle
facing-fazing
racing-raising
bracing-braising
gracing-grazing
ceasing-seizing
bussing-buzzing
racer-razor
maces-mazes
races-raises
prices-prizes
doses-dozes
buses-buzzes
lacy-lazy
gristly-grizzly

final
peace-peas

face-faze
lace-lays
place-plays
mace-maze
pace-pays
race-rays
brace-brays
grace-graze
trace-trays
fleece-fleas
niece-knees
ice-eyes
dice-dies
lice-lies
spice-spies
rice-rise
price-prize
pence-pens

since-sins
fierce-fears
pierce-peers
force-fours
source-sores
sauce-saws
deuce-dues
base-bays
cease-seize
dense-dens
dose-doze
loose-lose
loss-laws
floss-flaws
fuss-fuzz
bus-buzz

SOUND	VOICING	DURATION	PASSAGE	ARTICULATOR	POINT OF ARTICULATION
[č] chatter	voiceless	affricate	oral	front of tongue	hard palate
[š] shatter	voiceless	continuant	oral	front of tongue	hard palate

Languages

Arabic
Cebuano
Danish
Estonian
Fijian
Finnish
Greek
Hausa
Hawaiian
Javanese
Korean
Marshallese
Persian
Portuguese
Samoan
Spanish
Swahili
Swedish
Tagalog
Tamil
Thai
Tongan
Vietnamese

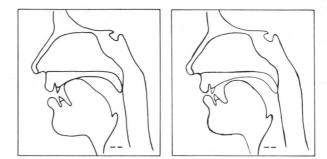

SENTENCES WITH CONTEXTUAL CLUES

(init.)   There's a CHERRY in my SHERRY.
         Those SHEEP are not CHEAP.
(med.)   Do WITCHES grant WISHES?
(fin.)   We can't MARCH in that MARSH.
         There is too MUCH of that MUSH.

MINIMAL SENTENCES

(init.)   I heard something CHATTER/SHATTER.
         He bumped his CHIN/SHIN.
(med.)   There is water in the DITCHES/DISHES.
         He is WATCHING/WASHING it.
(fin.)   Please MATCH/MASH them.

initial
chaffed-shaft
chair-share
chaired-shared
chant-shan't
chanty-shanty
chatter-shatter
chattered-shattered
chatterer-shatterer
chattering-shattering
cheap-sheep
cheat-sheet
cheating-sheeting
cheddar-shedder
cheek-sheik
cheer-sheer
cheese-she's
cherry-sherry
chew-shoe
chewed-shoed
chewing-shoeing
chide-shied

chief-sheaf
chill-shill
chilling-shilling
chin-shin
chip-ship
chipped-shipped
chipper-shipper
chock-shock
chocked-shocked
choose-shoes
chop-shop
chopped-shopped
chopper-shopper
chopping-shopping
chore-shore
chose-shows
chuck-shuck
chucked-shucked
chucking-shucking

medial
hatched-hashed

latched-lashed
matched-mashed
watched-washed
ditched-dished
switched-swished
leeching-leashing
catching-cashing
hatching-hashing
latching-lashing
matching-mashing
watching-washing
ditching-dishing
switching-swishing
matcher-masher
watcher-washer
leeches-leashes
marches-marshes
batches-bashes
catches-cashes
hatches-hashes
latches-lashes
matches-mashes

watches-washes
ditches-dishes
witches-wishes
switches-swishes
crutches-crushes

final
leech-leash
which-whish
march-marsh
batch-bash
catch-cash
hatch-hash
latch-lash
match-mash
watch-wash
ditch-dish
witch-wish
switch-swish
Butch-bush
hutch-hush
crutch-crush

SOUND	VOICING	DURATION	PASSAGE	ARTICULATOR	POINT OF ARTICULATION
[ǰ] Jack	voiced	affricate	oral	front of tongue	hard palate
[š] shack	voiceless	continuant	oral	front of tongue	hard palate

Languages

Arabic
  (final)
Estonian
Fijian
Finnish
Hawaiian
Hebrew
Indonesian
Korean
Marshallese
Portuguese
Samoan
Spanish
Thai
Tongan
Vietnamese

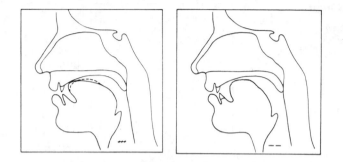

SENTENCES WITH CONTEXTUAL CLUES

(init.) It will JELL in the SHELL.
         The JACK is in the SHACK.
         The SHEEP are in the JEEP.
(med.)   We were GYPPED when it was SHIPPED.
(fin.)   Is MARGE in the MARSH?

MINIMAL SENTENCES

(init.) I can hear them JINGLING/SHINGLING.
         Is that a JEEP/SHEEP coming?
         That's my GIN/SHIN.
(med.)   There was no MARGIN/MARTIAN.
(fin.)   It is SLUDGE/SLUSH.

initial			*medial*
gene-sheen	Jake-shake	Jerry-sherry	unjelled-unshelled
gin-shin	jam-sham	Jew-shoe	adjure-assure
gyp-ship	James-shames	jill-shill	ravaging-ravishing
gypped-shipped	jay-shay	jingled-shingled	margin-Martian
gypper-shipper	jeep-sheep	jingling-shingling	badges-bashes
gypping-shipping	jeer-sheer	Joan-shone	
jack-shack	jeered-sheared	jot-shot	*final*
jackal-shackle	jeering-shearing	jurist-surest	badge-bash
jade-shade	jell-shell	juror-surer	cadge-cash
jaded-shaded	jelled-shelled	jut-shut	fledge-flesh
jag-shag	jelling-shelling	jute-shoot	sludge-slush
jail-shale	jerk-shirk	jutting-shutting	Marge-marsh

SOUND	VOICING	DURATION	PASSAGE	ARTICULATOR	POINT OF ARTICULATION
[ɟ] jest	voiced	affricate	oral	front of tongue	hard palate
[z] zest	voiced	continuant	oral	tip of tongue	tooth ridge

Languages

Finnish
Hebrew
Indonesian
Javanese
Kannada
Portuguese
Tamil

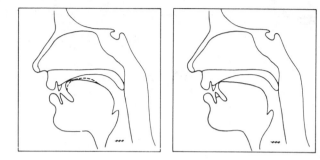

SENTENCES WITH CONTEXTUAL CLUES

(init.) Is JOAN in this ZONE?
He made the JEST with ZEST.
(med.) He GAUGES while he GAZES.
(fin.) He PAYS for each PAGE.
The CHAINS do not CHANGE.

MINIMAL SENTENCES

(init.) Were they GYPPED/ZIPPED?
He's a JEALOUS/ZEALOUS lover.
(med.) This tastes FUDGY/FUZZY.
(fin.) It depends on the RANGE/RAINS.
The BARGE/BARS stayed afloat.

initial
gee-Z
gyp-zip
gypped-zipped
gypper-zipper
gypping-zipping
jag-zag
jealous-zealous
jest-zest
jig-zig
jillion-zillion
jinks-zincs
Joan-zone
juice-Zeus

jute-zoot

medial
raged-raised
gauged-gazed
budged-buzzed
fragile-frazzle
raging-raising
budging-buzzing
gauging-gazing
budges-buzzes
sieges-seizes
fudgy-fuzzy

final
age-A's
cage-Kay's
carriage-carries
marriage-marries
page-pays
rage-rays
storage-stories
courage-curries
stage-stays
wage-ways
budge-buzz
fudge-fuzz
change-chains

range-rains
arrange-arraigns
strange-strains
binge-bins
singe-sins
tinge-tins
twinge-twins
barge-bars
charge-chars
forge-fours
purge-purrs
surge-sirs
gauge-gaze
huge-hues

SOUND	VOICING	DURATION	PASSAGE	ARTICULATOR	POINT OF ARTICULATION
[ǰ] jest	voiced	affricate	oral	front of tongue	hard palate
[č] chest	voiceless	affricate	oral	front of tongue	hard palate

Languages

Arabic
Cebuano
Czech
  (final)
Estonian
Fijian
Finnish
German
Hawaiian
Hebrew
Indonesian
Italian
Korean
Marshallese
Norwegian
Portuguese
Russian
Samoan
Spanish
Swahili
Swedish
Tagalog
Tamil
Thai
  (final)
Tongan
Vietnamese

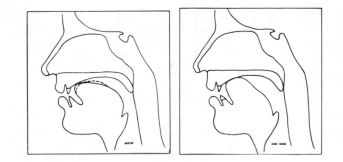

SENTENCES WITH CONTEXTUAL CLUES

(init.) The JEEP was not CHEAP.
        These CHERRIES are JERRY'S.
(med.) There are RICHES in those RIDGES.
(fin.) Was MARGE going to MARCH?
        She is in SEARCH of a blue SERGE.

MINIMAL SENTENCES

(init.) The crowd JEERED/CHEERED.
        He was JOKING/CHOKING.
(med.) It was a fine EDGING/ETCHING.
(fin.) It was a PURGE/PERCH.
        Did you see her LUNGE/LUNCH?

initial
gin-chin
gyp-chip
gypped-chipped
gypper-chipper
gypping-chipping
Jane-chain
jar-char
jarred-charred
jarring-charring
jeep-cheap
jeer-cheer
jeered-cheered
jeerer-cheerer
jeering-cheering

Jerry-cherry
jest-chest
jigger-chigger
Jill-chill
jinx-chinks
jitter-chitter
joke-choke
joked-choked
joker-choker
joking-choking
Joyce-choice
jug-chug
jugged-chugged
jugging-chugging
junk-chunk

junked-chunked
junking-chunking

medial
singeing-cinching
edging-etching
lunging-lunching
purging-perching
surging-searching
badges-batches
edges-etches
ridges-riches
bridges-britches
singes-cinches
lunges-lunches

surges-searches

final
badge-batch
cadge-catch
Madge-match
edge-etch
ridge-rich
singe-cinch
lunge-lunch
large-larch
Marge-march
purge-perch
surge-search

SOUND	VOICING	DURATION	PASSAGE	ARTICULATOR	POINT OF ARTICULATION
[j] jam	voiced	affricate	oral	front of tongue	hard palate
[y] yam	voiced	continuant	oral	front of tongue	hard palate

Languages

Estonian
Finnish
Greek
Hebrew
Indonesian
Micronesian
Norwegian
Persian
Portuguese
Spanish
Swahili
Swedish
Thai

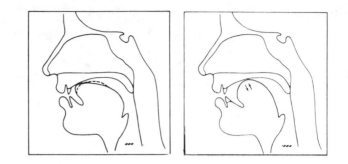

SENTENCES WITH CONTEXTUAL CLUES

(init.)   Is the JET here YET?
A bad YOLK is no JOKE.
It JARRED our whole YARD.
(med.)   They WEDGED it and WEIGHED it.
(fin.)   It LAY on the LEDGE.

MINIMAL SENTENCES

(init.)   JELLO/YELLOW is my favorite.
I like sweet JAMS/YAMS.
It was an unpleasant JEER/YEAR.
(med.)   They were PLEDGING/PLAYING.
(fin.)   Give it to MIDGE/ME.

initial
gyp-yip
gypped-yipped
gypper-yipper
gypping-yipping
jack-yak
jail-Yale
jam-yam
jarred-yard
jaw-yaw

jawed-yawed
jawing-yawing
Jay-yea
jeer-year
jell-yell
jelled-yelled
jelling-yelling
Jello-yellow
Jess-yes
jet-yet

jewel-you'll
John-yawn
joke-yolk
jot-yacht
jotting-yachting
jowl-yowl
juice-use

medial
wedged-weighed

pledging-playing
wedging-weighing
wedger-weigher

final
hedge-hay
ledge-lay
pledge-play
Midge-me
fridge-free

SOUND	VOICING	DURATION	PASSAGE	ARTICULATOR	POINT OF ARTICULATION
[g] bag	voiced	stop	oral	back of tongue	soft palate
[ŋ] bang	voiced	continuant	nasal	back of tongue	soft palate

Languages

Fijian
Georgian
Hebrew
Japanese
  (medial)
Polish
Tamil
Urdu
Vietnamese

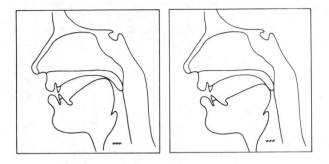

SENTENCES WITH CONTEXTUAL CLUES

(med.) He can't JUGGLE in the JUNGLE.
  The costumer made WIGS to match the WINGS.
(fin.) That LOG is LONG.
  The GANG used a GAG.
  Pick a SPRIG at the SPRING.

MINIMAL SENTENCES

(med.) JIGGLE/JINGLE the bell.
  She doesn't look good with those BAGS/BANGS.
  The man is a STRAGGLER/STRANGLER.
(fin.) Is that why they SAG/SANG?
  Stand on the first RUG/RUNG.

medial
bagging-banging
gagging-ganging
rigging-ringing
bogging-bonging
bagger-banger
digger-dinger
rigor-ringer
bags-bangs
fags-fangs
gags-gangs
hags-hangs
rigs-rings
sprigs-springs
wigs-wings
logs-longs
lugs-lungs
rugs-rungs
tugs-tongues

final
bag-bang
fag-fang
gag-gang
hag-hang
slag-slang
rag-rang
sag-sang
tag-tang
pig-ping
rig-ring
sprig-spring
wig-wing
dug-dung
hug-hung
lug-lung
slug-slung
rug-rung

73

SOUND	VOICING	DURATION	PASSAGE	ARTICULATOR	POINT OF ARTICULATION
[g] gap	voiced	stop	oral	back of tongue	soft palate
[k] cap	voiceless	stop	oral	back of tongue	soft palate

Languages

Arabic
  (final)
Estonian
Fijian
Finnish
German
  (final)
Hawaiian
Indonesian
Italian
Korean
Marshallese
Micronesian
Samoan
Tamil
Thai
  (final)
Tongan
Vietnamese
  (final)

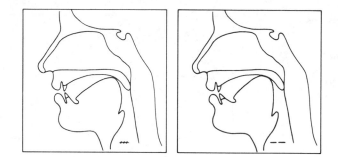

SENTENCES WITH CONTEXTUAL CLUES

(init.)   They CAME for the GAME.
          The GOLD feels COLD.
          You COULD do some GOOD.
(med.)   The acrobat's ANKLES form strange ANGLES.
(fin.)   The DOG is on the DOCK.

MINIMAL SENTENCES

(init.)   It is a fine GAUZE/CAUSE.
          I think it will be GOLD/COLD.
(med.)   He is TAGGING/TACKING them.
(fin.)   Put it in the BAG/BACK.
          There's a SNAG/SNACK in my coat pocket.

initial
gable-cable
gad-cad
gain-cane
gaiter-cater
gall-call
game-came
gap-cap
gape-cape
gash-cash
gauge-cage
gauze-cause
gave-cave
ghost-coast
ghoul-cool
girdle-curdle
girl-curl
glad-clad
glamour-clamor
glass-class
glean-clean
glows-close
glue-clue

goal-coal
goat-coat
gob-cob
gold-cold
good-could
gore-core
got-cot
grab-crab
graft-craft
grain-crane
gram-cram
grape-crepe
grass-crass
grate-crate
grave-crave
graze-craze
grease-crease
greater-crater
greed-creed
grouch-crouch
grow-crow
guard-card
gum-come

gutter-cutter
medial
ungashed-uncashed
ungapped-uncapped
ungored-uncored
preglued-preclude
degree-decree
pregrease-precrease
bagging-backing
sagging-sacking
tagging-tacking
pegging-pecking
clogging-clocking
plugging-plucking
tugging-tucking
regain-recane
bigger-bicker
piggy-picky
muggy-mucky

final
league-leak
bag-back

hag-hack
shag-shack
lag-lack
slag-slack
nag-knack
snag-snack
rag-rack
crag-crack
sag-sack
tag-tack
stag-stack
wag-Wac
peg-peck
pig-pick
brig-brick
prig-prick
wig-wick
hog-hock
frog-frock
bug-buck
dug-duck
lug-luck

MULTIPLE CONTRASTS

Front Vowels

[iy]	[i]	[ey]	[e]	[æ]	[iy]	[i]	[ey]	[e]	[æ]
bead	bid	bayed	bed	bad	bean	bin	bane	Ben	ban
lead	lid	laid	led	lad	dean	din	dane	den	Dan
deed	did	----	dead	dad	keen	kin	cane	Ken	can
heed	hid	----	head	had	teen	tin	----	ten	tan
meed	mid	maid	----	mad	reap	rip	rape	rep	rap
reed	rid	raid	red	----	he's	his	haze	----	has
greed	grid	grade	----	grad	eat	it	ate	----	at
beak	----	bake	beck	back	beat	bit	bait	bet	bat
leak	lick	lake	----	lack	heat	hit	hate	----	hat
peak	pick	----	peck	pack	meat	mit	mate	met	mat
reek	rick	rake	wreck	rack	neat	knit	Nate	net	gnat
deal	dill	dale	dell	----	peat	pit	pate	pet	pat
peal	pill	pail	----	pal	seat	sit	sate	set	sat
seal	sill	sail	sell	Sal	feet	fit	fate	----	fat
feel	fill	fail	fell	----	sleet	slit	slate	----	slat
heel	hill	hail	hell	Hal	feast	fist	faced	----	fast
deem	dim	dame	----	dam	least	list	laced	lest	last

Back Vowels

[uw]	[u]	[ə]	[ow]
shooed	should	----	showed
booed	----	bud	bowed
cooed	could	cud	code
wooed	wood	----	----
stewed	stood	stud	stowed
who'd	hood	----	hoed
mood	----	mud	mowed
crude	----	crud	crowed
rune	----	run	roan
tune	----	ton	tone
Luke	look	luck	----
cool	----	cull	coal
fool	full	----	foal
pool	pull	----	pole
ghoul	----	gull	goal
doom	----	dumb	dome
noon	----	nun	known
coop	----	cup	cope
hoop	----	hup	hope
soup	----	sup	soap
boot	----	but	boat
boost	----	bust	boast
roost	----	rust	roast

Diphthongs

[iy]	[ey]	[uw]	[ow]	[ay]	[aw]	[oy]
----	----	----	----	ply	plow	ploy
plea	play	pooh	----	pie	pow	poi
pea	pay	sue	so	sigh	sow	soy
sea	say	too	toe	tie	----	toy
tea	----	boo	bow	buy	bow	boy
bee	bay	who	ho	high	how	----
he	hay	flew	flow	fly	----	----
flee	flay	----	----	----	----	----
----	ray	rue	row	rye	row	Roy
bead	bade	booed	bode	bide	bowed	buoyed
lead	laid	lewd	load	lied	loud	Lloyd
read	raid	rude	road	ride	----	----
breed	braid	brood	----	bride	browed	----
speak	spake	spook	spoke	spike	----	----
eel	ale	----	----	isle	owl	oil
deal	dale	duel	dole	dial	----	Doyle
peal	pale	pool	pole	pile	Powell	----
real	rail	rule	role	rile	----	roil
teal	tail	tool	toll	tile	towel	toil
feel	fail	fool	foal	file	foul	foil
heel	hail	who'll	hole	----	howl	Hoyle
deem	dame	doom	dome	dime	----	----
Jean	Jane	June	Joan	----	----	join
lean	lane	loon	loan	line	----	loin
mean	mane	moon	moan	mine	----	----
keen	cane	coon	cone	kine	----	coin
beat	bait	boot	boat	bite	----	----

Lax Vowels

[i]	[e]	[æ]	[ə]	[a]	[u]	[ɔ]
pinned	penned	panned	punned	pond	——	pawned
bid	bed	bad	bud	——	——	bawd
did	dead	dad	dud	——	——	——
kid	——	cad	cud	cod	could	cawed
——	ped	pad	——	pod	——	pawed
middle	meddle	——	muddle	model	——	——
big	beg	bag	bug	bog	——	——
——	beck	back	buck	bock	book	balk
hick	heck	hack	huck	hock	hook	hawk
chick	check	——	chuck	chock	——	chalk
nick	neck	knack	——	knock	nook	——
pick	peck	pack	puck	pock	——	——
tick	tech	tack	tuck	tock	took	talk
stick	——	stack	stuck	stock	——	stalk
bill	bell	——	——	——	bull	ball
fill	fell	——	——	——	full	fall
bitter	better	batter	butter	——	——	——
miss	mess	mass	muss	——	——	moss
lift	left	laughed	luffed	——	——	loft
bit	bet	bat	but	bot	——	bought
kit	——	cat	cut	cot	——	caught
knit	net	gnat	nut	not	——	nought
pit	pet	pat	putt	pot	put	——
writ	ret	rat	rut	rot	——	wrought
sit	set	sat	——	sot	soot	sought

Clusters with [l] and [r]

band	bland	brand
bayed	blade	braid
bead	bleed	breed
bed	bled	bread
best	blest	breast
bite	blight	bright
boo	blue	brew
bunt	blunt	brunt
cash	clash	crash
caw	claw	craw
coo	clue	crew
fame	flame	frame
fed	fled	Fred
fee	flee	free
fight	flight	fright
gad	glad	grad
gas	glass	grass
gaze	glaze	graze
go	glow	grow
goat	gloat	groat
pants	plants	prance
pay	play	pray
peasant	pleasant	present
pie	ply	pry
pod	plod	prod

[w] Contrasted with [kw] and [kl]

Wac	quack	clack
wad	quad	clod
wail	quail	——
wake	quake	——
wart	quart	——
warts	quartz	——
wash	quash	——
waver	quaver	——
wean	queen	clean
well	quell	——
wench	quench	clench
west	quest	——
wick	quick	click
will	quill	——
wilt	quilt	——
wince	quince	——
wire	choir	——
wit	quit	——
work	quirk	clerk

[st] Contrasted with [zd]

faced	fazed
laced	lazed
raced	raised
priced	prized
ceased	seized
fussed	fuzzed
haste	hazed
east	eased
whist	whizzed
cost	caused
host	hosed
boost	boozed
post	posed
bust	buzzed

Clusters Ending with [d]

[d]	[ld]	[rd]	[nd]	[ŋd]	[md]	[bd]	[gd]	[vd]	[jd]	[zd]
bad	—	—	band	banged	—	—	bagged	—	badged	—
—	—	barred	bond	bonged	bombed	bobbed	bogged	—	—	—
cad	—	—	canned	—	—	—	—	calved	cadged	—
gad	—	—	—	ganged	—	gabbed	gagged	—	—	—
feed	field	feared	fiend	—	—	—	—	—	—	—
weed	wield	wierd	weaned	—	—	—	—	weaved	—	wheezed
hoed	hold	hoard	honed	—	homed	—	—	—	—	hosed
sewed	sold	soared	—	—	—	—	—	—	—	—
bowed	bold	bored	boned	—	—	—	—	—	—	—
heed	healed	—	—	—	—	—	—	heaved	—	—
aid	ailed	aired	—	—	aimed	—	—	—	aged	—
paid	paled	paired	pained	—	—	—	—	paved	paged	—
raid	railed	—	rained	—	—	—	—	raved	raged	raised
cod	—	card	conned	—	calmed	—	cogged	—	—	—
god	—	guard	—	gonged	—	—	—	—	—	—
laud	—	lord	lawned	longed	—	—	—	—	—	—
—	mild	mired	mind	—	mimed	—	—	—	—	—
bud	—	—	bunned	bunged	bummed	—	bugged	—	budged	buzzed
tide	tiled	tired	tined	—	timed	—	—	—	—	—
wide	wild	wired	wind	—	—	—	—	wived	—	wised
ode	old	—	owned	—	—	—	—	—	—	—
code	cold	cored	coned	—	combed	—	—	coved	—	—
—	fold	—	phoned	—	foamed	—	—	—	—	—

Clusters Beginning with [l]

[l]	[lz]	[ld]	[lt]	[lč]	[lf]	[lm]	[lk]	[lp]	[lθ]
mole	moles	mold	molt	—	—	—	—	—	—
coal	coals	cold	colt	—	—	—	—	—	—
el	els	—	—	—	elf	elm	elk	—	—
ball	balls	balled	—	—	—	—	—	—	—
call	calls	called	—	—	—	—	—	—	—
gall	galls	galled	—	—	—	—	—	—	—
hall	halls	hauled	halt	—	—	—	—	—	—
bell	bells	belled	belt	belch	—	—	—	—	—
hell	hells	held	—	—	—	helm	—	help	health
shell	shells	shelled	—	—	shelf	—	—	—	—
well	wells	weld	welt	Welch	—	—	—	whelp	wealth
yell	yells	yelled	—	—	—	—	—	yelp	—
fill	fills	filled	—	filch	—	film	—	—	filth
gill	gills	guild	guilt	—	—	—	—	—	—
mill	mills	milled	—	milch	—	—	milk	—	—
sill	sills	silled	silt	—	—	—	silk	—	—
gull	gulls	gulled	—	gulch	gulf	—	—	gulp	—
pull	pulls	pulled	—	—	—	—	—	—	—
maul	mauls	mauled	malt	—	—	—	—	—	—
bowl	bowls	bowled	bolt	—	—	—	—	—	—

Clusters Beginning with [s]

[s]	[sl]	[sp]	[spr]	[st]	[str]	[sn]	[sm]	[sw]	[sk]	[skw]
sack	slack	—	—	stack	—	snack	smack	—	—	—
sag	slag	—	—	stag	—	snag	—	swag	—	—
said	sled	sped	spread	stead	—	—	—	—	—	—
sake	slake	spake	—	stake	strake	snake	—	—	—	—
sand	—	spanned	—	stand	strand	—	—	—	scanned	—
sane	slain	Spain	sprain	stain	strain	—	—	swain	skein	—
sans	—	spans	—	Stan's	—	—	—	—	scans	—
sap	slap	—	—	—	strap	snap	—	—	—	—
—	—	spare	—	stare	—	snare	—	swear	scare	square
sat	slat	spat	sprat	—	—	—	—	—	scat	—
Saul	—	—	sprawl	stall	—	—	small	—	—	squall
say	slay	spay	spray	stay	stray	—	—	sway	—	—
sear	—	spear	—	steer	—	sneer	smear	—	—	—
seed	—	speed	—	steed	—	—	—	Swede	skied	—
seek	sleek	speak	—	—	streak	sneak	—	—	—	squeak
seep	sleep	—	—	steep	—	—	—	sweep	—	—
sicker	slicker	—	—	sticker	—	snicker	—	—	—	—
side	slide	spied	—	—	stride	snide	—	—	—	—
sigh	sly	spy	spry	sty	—	—	—	—	sky	—
sight	slight	spite	sprite	—	—	—	smite	—	—	—
sill	—	spill	—	still	—	—	—	swill	skill	—
sing	sling	—	spring	sting	string	—	—	swing	—	—
sip	slip	—	—	—	strip	snip	—	—	skip	—
sit	slit	spit	sprit	—	—	—	—	—	skit	—
so	slow	—	—	stow	—	snow	—	—	—	—
soak	—	spoke	—	stoke	stroke	—	smoke	—	—	—
sob	slob	—	—	—	—	snob	—	swab	—	squab
sot	slot	spot	—	—	—	—	—	swat	Scot	squat
sum	slum	—	—	—	strum	—	—	swum	scum	—
sunk	slunk	spunk	—	stunk	—	—	—	—	skunk	—

Clusters Ending with [s]

[s]	[ps]	[ts]	[fs]	[ks]	[nts]	[mps]	[θs]	[sts]	[sks]
—	caps	oats	—	—	cants	camps	—	casts	casks
—	reaps	—	reefs	reeks	—	—	wreaths	—	—
lass	laps	—	laughs	lacks	—	lamps	laths	lasts	—
class	claps	—	—	clacks	—	clamps	—	—	—
—	flaps	flats	—	flax	—	—	—	—	flasks
—	slaps	slats	—	slacks	slants	—	—	—	—
mass	maps	mats	—	Mack's	—	—	—	masts	masks
—	raps	rats	—	racks	rants	ramps	—	—	—
—	cheeps	cheats	chiefs	cheeks	—	—	—	—	—
—	sheeps	sheets	—	sheik's	—	—	sheaths	—	—
hiss	hips	hits	—	hicks	hints	—	—	—	—
—	lips	—	—	licks	lints	limps	—	lists	—
—	clips	—	cliffs	clicks	Clint's	—	—	—	—
—	tips	—	tiffs	ticks	tints	—	—	—	—
bus	—	butts	buffs	bucks	bunts	bumps	—	busts	—
—	—	huts	huffs	Huck's	hunts	humps	—	—	husks

Clusters Ending with [t]

[t]	[pt]	[ft]	[st]	[kt]	[čt]
ate	aped	——	aced	ached	——
fate	——	——	faced	faked	——
Kate	caped	——	cased	caked	——
rate	raped	——	raced	raked	——
wrote	roped	——	roast	——	——
at	apt	aft	——	act	——
bat	——	——	——	backed	batched
peat	peeped	——	pieced	peeked	——
coat	coped	——	coast	coked	coached
moat	moped	——	most	——	——
rat	rapped	raft	——	racked	——
beet	beeped	beefed	beast	beaked	beached
let	——	left	lest	——	——
wet	wept	weft	west	——	——
hit	hipped	——	hissed	——	hitched
writ	ripped	rift	wrist	——	——
sit	sipped	sift	cyst	sicked	——
cot	copped	——	——	cocked	——
lot	lopped	——	——	locked	——

Clusters Beginning with [m] or [n]

[mp]	[mps]	[mpt]	[nt]	[nts]	[nd]	[nz]	[ndz]
amp	amps	——	ant	ants	and	Ann's	——
camp	camps	camped	cant	cants	canned	cans	——
scamp	scamps	scamped	scant	——	scanned	scans	——
champ	champs	champed	chant	chants	——	scans	——
——	——	——	plant	plants	planned	plans	——
——	——	——	meant	——	mend	men's	mends
——	——	——	pant	pants	panned	pans	——
ramp	ramps	——	rant	rants	——	——	——
——	——	——	lent	——	lend	lens	lends
——	——	——	——	wince	wind	wins	winds
——	——	——	sent	scents	send	——	sends
limp	limps	limped	lint	lints	——	——	——
bump	bumps	bumped	bunt	bunts	bunned	buns	——
hump	humps	humped	hunt	hunts	——	Huns	——
pump	pumps	pumped	punt	punts	punned	puns	——
rump	rumps	rumped	runt	runts	——	runs	——
stump	stumps	stumped	stunt	stunts	stunned	stuns	——

Clusters Ending with [z]

[z]	[dz]	[gz]	[mz]	[nz]	[ŋz]	[lz]	[rz]	[ndz]	[vz]
raise	raids	—	—	rains	—	rails	—	—	raves
rose	roads	rogues	roams	roans	—	rolls	—	—	roves
has	—	hags	hams	—	hangs	—	—	hands	halves
laws	lauds	logs	—	lawns	longs	lolls	—	—	—
sees	seeds	—	seems	scenes	—	seals	—	—	—
ties	tides	—	times	tines	—	tiles	tires	—	—
—	cods	cogs	—	cons	—	—	cars	—	—
—	—	wigs	—	wins	wings	wills	—	winds	—
—	—	bogs	bombs	—	bongs	balls	bars	bonds	—
—	pods	—	—	—	—	—	pars	ponds	—
stows	—	—	—	stones	—	stoles	—	—	stoves
trays	trades	—	—	trains	—	trails	—	—	—
—	beds	begs	—	Ben's	—	bells	—	bends	—
—	—	bags	—	bans	bangs	—	—	bands	—
—	lads	lags	lambs	—	—	—	—	lands	—
—	—	sags	Sam's	sans	—	—	—	sands	salves
jazz	—	jags	jams	Jan's	—	—	—	—	—
fizz	—	figs	—	fins	—	fills	fears	—	—
buzz	buds	bugs	bums	buns	bungs	—	—	—	—

GLOSSARY

AFFRICATE: A consonant which is made up of two or more basic sounds — a stop followed by a homorganic continuant. The words *chin* and *gin* begin with affricates. The first word begins with /č/, which can be broken down into /t/ and /š/. The second word begins with /j/, which can be broken down into /d/ and /ž/. See the consonant chart on page ix.

ARTICULATOR: The most movable speech organs, i.e. the bottom lip, tongue tip, tongue mid, tongue back.

BACK VOWEL: A vowel which is pronounced with the back part of the tongue higher than the rest of the tongue. The words *cooed*, *could*, *code*, and *cawed* contain back vowels. See the vowel on page viii.

CENTRAL VOWEL: A vowel which is pronounced with the central part of the tongue higher than the tip or back of the tongue. The words *cut* and *cot* contain central vowels. See the vowel chart on page viii.

CONSONANT CLUSTER: Consonants occurring together, with no intervening vowel, e.g. /sl-/ or /-rp/. English has a great many consonant clusters which are difficult for the learner of English as a foreign language. Consonant clusters should not be confused with single phonemes which happen to be written with more than one symbol in traditional orthography, such as <th>, <sh>, <ph>, etc.

CONTEXTUAL CLUES: The structure of the sentence is such that it helps the student distinguish between minimal contrasts. For example, in the sentence, "Did they VOTE on the BOAT?" the word *vote* has the position of a verb, i.e. following the auxiliary *did* and the pronoun subject *they*, while the word *boat* has the position of a noun, i.e. following the preposition *on* and the determiner *the*. In the sentences which contain contextual clues, the two words under consideration cannot be reversed; if they could be reversed, the contextual clues would be of little help.

CONTINUANT: A consonant which can be pronounced continuously. The words *white*, *fight*, *thigh*, *sight*, *shy*, *high*, *Y*, *vie*, *thy*, *Zion*, *lie*, *rye*, *Zsa Zsa*, *my*, and *night* all begin with continuants. *Ping* ends with a continuant. Another word for *continuant* is *fricative*. See the consonant chart on page ix.

CONTRAST: See *minimal pair*.

DIPHTHONGIZATION: The changing of the speech organs during the production of a vowel sound. The vowels in *bit*, *bet*, *bat*, *but*, *cot*, *caught*, and *put* are not diphthongized; the vowels in *beat*, and *boot* are slightly diphthongized; the vowels in *bait*, and *boat* are definitely diphthongized; and the vowels in *buy*, *bough*, and *boy* are greatly diphthongized. Another word for diphthong is *glide*.

FRICATIVE: See *continuant*.

FRONT VOWEL: A vowel which is pronounced with the tip of the tongue higher than the rest of the tongue. The words *beat*, *bit*, *bait*, *bet*, and *bat* contain front vowels. See the vowel chart on page viii.

GLIDE: See *diphthong*.

HARD PALATE: The hard part of the roof of the mouth, which corresponds to the middle of the tongue. See *point of articulation*.

HIGH VOWEL: A vowel which is pronounced with some part of the tongue in a high position. The words *leak*, *lick*, *Luke*, and *look* contain high vowels. See the vowel chart on page viii.

HOMORGANIC SOUNDS: Two or more sounds pronounced one after the other with the organs of speech in approximately the same position.

HORIZONTAL POSITION: A description, in the production of vowels, of the position of the highest part of the tongue as being in the front, mid, or back part of the mouth. See the vowel chart on page viii.

JUNCTURE: The way in which sounds are separated. There is word juncture between the /t/ and /r/ of *night rate*, but not *nitrate*. An unfinished sentence ends with one kind of juncture, a question ends with another kind, and a regular statement ends with still another kind.

LAX VOWEL: A vowel which is pronounced with the muscles of the throat and tongue lax. The words *pit, pet, put, pot,* and *putt* contain lax vowels. See the vowel chart on page viii.

LIP ROUNDING: See *rounded vowel.*

LOW VOWEL: A vowel which is pronounced with the highest part of the tongue in a low position. The words *cat, cot,* and *caught* contain low vowels. See the vowel chart on page viii.

MANNER OF ARTICULATION: A description of whether a particular sound is a stop, continuant, or affricate; whether it is voiced or voiceless; whether it is oral, or nasal, etc.

MID VOWEL: A vowel which is pronounced with the highest part of the tongue in a mid (neither high nor low) position. The words *bait, bet, but,* and *boat* contain mid vowels. See the vowel chart on page viii.

MINIMAL PAIR: Two words which are pronounced the same except for a single sound, e.g. *bet-bat.* In the example given, the two vowel sounds are separate phonemes because they are significantly distinctive, i.e. the difference between the two words must be due to different vowels, since the rest of the two words is the same (b-t). Another term for minimal pairs is *minimal contrast.*

MINIMAL SENTENCES: Two sentences which are pronounced the same except for a single phoneme. Not only must the phonemes of the two sentences be the same, but the stress, intonation, juncture, etc. must also be the same for the sentences to be minimal.

NASAL: A sound which is pronounced with the velic open so that the air is allowed to go through the nasal cavity; see *point of articulation.* The words *simmer, sinner,* and *singer* contain nasals as their middle consonants. See the consonant chart on page ix.

ORAL: A sound which is pronounced with the velic closed so that air is forced to go only through the mouth (as opposed to going through the nasal cavity). See *point of articulation.* All English vowels and continuants are generally oral, except /m/, /n/, and /ŋ/. See the consonant chart on page ix.

PHONEME: The smallest unit of significantly distinctive sound. In English, the vowel sound in *beat* and that in *bit* are two separate phonemes, whereas in Spanish (for example), the two vowel sounds are not significantly different (and generally not distinctive), and are therefore not separate phonemes.

PHONEMIC ALPHABET: An alphabet which accurately reflects all and only the significant sound differences of a language, i.e. an alphabet which contains one and only one symbol for every significant sound (phoneme). See the vowel and consonant charts on pages viii and ix for an example of a phonemic alphabet.

PHONETIC ENVIRONMENT: The sounds immediately preceding and following the phoneme under consideration. The phonetic environment generally influences the quality of a particular sound; thus the vowel sound of *man* is nasalized because it is preceded by and followed by nasals, whereas the vowel sound of *bad* is not nasalized. Nevertheless, the vowel sounds of *man* and *bad* belong to the same phoneme /æ/. The phonetic environment also influences the quantity, i.e. duration, of sounds; thus the vowel sound in *cat* is much shorter than the vowel sound in *cans,* although again both sounds belong to the same phenome /æ/.

POINT OF ARTICULATION: The point at which the articulator touches **or** nearly touches during the production of a particular sound. In order to identify the points of articulation, as well as articulators, air passages, etc., the following diagram may be helpful.

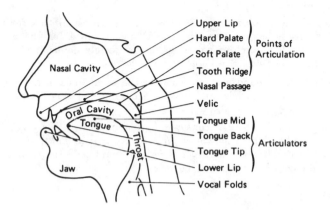

ROUNDED VOWEL: A vowel which is pronounced with the lips rounded. In English, only the back vowels are rounded, and the higher vowels are rounded more than the lower ones. The words *cooed, could, code,* and *cawed* contain rounded vowels. The vowel in the word *low* begins unrounded and becomes rounded during its production. The vowel in *boy* begins rounded and becomes unrounded during its production. See the vowel chart on page viii.

SEMI-CONSONANT: A consonant which can act as a vowel. For example, the last syllable of the word *button* can be pronounced without a regular vowel, i.e. without moving the tongue away from the tooth ridge between the production of /t/ and /n/. Since every syllable must contain a vowel (or vocalic segment), and since there is no regular vowel in the second syllable of some pronunciations of *button*, the /n/ must function as a vowel. Any consonant which can thus function is a semi-consonant.

SOFT PALATE: The soft part of the roof of the mouth, which corresponds to the back of the tongue. See *point of articulation.*

STOP: A consonant which must be pronounced instantaneously. The words *pie, buy, tie, dye, Kai,* and *guy* all begin with stops. See the consonant chart on page xi.

STRESS POSITION: That position which contains a stressed word. A stressed word in English is generally pronounced with greater intensity (loudness), higher pitch, and greater duration (length of time) on its most prominent syllable.

TENSE VOWEL: A vowel which is pronounced with the muscles of the throat and tongue tense. The words *beat, bait, bat, boot, boat, bought, bite, bout* and *boy* contain tense vowels. See the vowel chart on page viii.

TOOTH RIDGE: A small ridge just behind the top teeth. See *point of articulation.*

TRADITIONAL ORTHOGRAPHY: The spelling system generally used for writing English.

UNROUNDED VOWEL: A vowel which is pronounced with the lips unrounded. The words *beat, bit, bait, bet, bat, but, cot,* and *bite* contain unrounded vowels. See also *rounded vowel.*

VELIC: A movable appendage at the extreme back of the roof of the mouth which is able to close off the air so that it cannot go through the nasal cavity. See *point of articulation.*

VERTICAL POSITION: A description, in the production of vowels, of the position of the highest part of the tongue as being near the top of the mouth, in the middle of the mouth, or near the bottom of the mouth. See the vowel chart on page viii.

VOCAL FOLDS: Appendages in the throat which can remain lax for the production of voiceless sounds and which can become tense for the production of voiced sounds. The pitch of voiced sounds is largely determined by the tenseness of the vocal folds. See *point of articulation.*

VOICED SOUND: A sound pronounced with the vocal folds in the larynx vibrating. In English all vowels, and most consonants and clusters are voiced. See *point of articulation.* See also page ix.

VOICELESS CONSONANT: A consonant pronounced with the vocal folds in the larynx not vibrating. The words *pie, tie, Kai, why, fight, thigh, sigh, shy, high,* and *chide* all begin with voiceless consonants. See *point of articulation.* See also the consonant chart on page ix.

LANGUAGE INDEX

THAI: 1, 5, 7-8, 13, 16, 18-21, 23, 35-36, 39-40, 43, 50-51, 54-57, 60, 65, 68-69, 71-72, 74.

TONGAN: 1, 8, 12-13, 15-16, 18-19, 21, 24, 27, 35-37, 44, 51-56, 61, 64, 66-69, 71, 74.

TURKISH: 1, 8, 12, 16, 18, 23-25, 27, 35-36, 39-40, 44, 51, 54-55, 58.

URDU: 1-6, 8-17, 20-28, 30-34, 38-42, 44, 49, 51-56, 58, 73.

UZBEK: 8, 12, 16, 36, 39, 44, 51, 54.

VIETNAMESE: 1, 3, 5, 8, 12, 16, 18-20, 23-24, 27, 35-36, 39, 43-46, 49, 51-57, 60, 65-69, 71, 73-74.

What are you plans for the future?